Complete Rhapsodies
and Other Works for Solo Piano

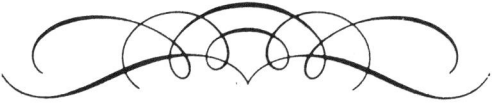

Ernő Dohnányi

Notes by Robert Rimm

DOVER PUBLICATIONS, INC.
Mineola, New York

Copyright

Copyright © 1999 by Dover Publications, Inc.
All rights reserved under Pan American and International Copyright Conventions.

Bibliographical Note

This Dover edition, first published in 1999, is a new compilation of works originally published separately. Ludwig Doblinger (Bernhard Herzmansky), Leipzig, originally published *Passacaglia,* Op. 6, 1904, and *Vier Rhapsodien,* Op. 11, n.d. Rózsavölgyi & Co. [Budapest] originally published three works in this collection: *Hat Koncertetűd,* Op. 28, 1916; *Variációk egy magyar népdalra,* Op. 29, 1917; and *Pastorale,* 1922. *Winterreigen,* Op. 13, and *Humoresken,* Op. 17, are reproduced from authoritative early editions, n.d.

Robert Rimm's introductory notes to the Dover edition were prepared specially for this publication, as was Stanley Appelbaum's English translation of titles and of the poem "Winterreigen." In its original publication, Viktor Heindl's poem, in German only, appeared as a preface to Dohnányi's suite; it is positioned here as a postscript to provide the player with a practical layout of the music.

For providing the original edition of *Vier Rhapsodien* for this publication, we are indebted to the International Piano Archives at Maryland, University of Maryland, and its Curator, Professor Donald Manildi.

International Standard Book Number: 0-486-40618-0

Manufactured in the United States of America
Dover Publications, Inc., 31 East 2nd Street, Mineola, N.Y. 11501

Contents

Introductory notes　*v*

Passacaglia, Op. 6 (1899). 1

Vier Rhapsodien, Op. 11, Nos. 1–4 (1902–3) 28
[*Four Rhapsodies*]
  Rhapsody No. 1 in G Minor 28
  Rhapsody No. 2 in F-sharp Minor 45
  Rhapsody No. 3 in C Major 56
  Rhapsody No. 4 in E-flat Minor 67

Winterreigen, Op. 13 (1905). 78
[*Winter Rounds: 10 Bagatelles*]
  1. Widmung • *Dedication* 78
  2. Marsch der lustigen Brüder • *March of the merry companions* 80
  3. An Ada • *To Ada* 84
  4. Freund Victor's Mazurka • *My friend Victor's mazurka* 85
  5. Sphärenmusik • *Music of the spheres* 90
  6. Valse aimable • *Charming waltz* 97
  7. Um Mitternacht • *At midnight* 100
  8. Tolle Gesellschaft • *Wild party* 104
  9. Morgengrauen • *Daybreak* 110
  10. Postludium 112
  — Poem: *Winterreigen* (Viktor Heindl) 114

Humoresken in Form einer Suite, Op. 17 (1907). 115
[*Humoresques in the form of a suite*]
  1. Marsch • *March* 115
  2. Toccata 121
  3. Pavane aus dem 16. Jahrhundert mit Variationem
    • *Pavane from the 16th century with variations* 131
  4. Pastorale 140
  5. Introduction und Fuge • *Introduction and fugue* 146

Sechs Konzertetüden, Op. 28 (1916) 160
[*Six concert etudes*]
  1. In A Minor 160
  2. In D-flat Major 166
  3. In E-flat Minor 170
  4. In B-flat Minor 181
  5. In E Major 191
  6. Capriccio in F Minor 201

Variationen über ein ungarisches Volkslied, Op. 29 (1917) 209
[*Variations on a Hungarian folk song*]

Pastorale: "Mennyből az angyal" (1920) 222
[*Pastorale on the Hungarian Christmas song "The angel is from heaven"*]

INTRODUCTION

Born in Hungary in 1877, Ernő Dohnányi belonged to the same fertile generation that produced Bartók, Ravel, Schoenberg, Stravinsky and others who formed the backbone of early 20th-century composition. Those who came of age in the early 1900s witnessed the first masterpieces of free atonality, impressionism and radical dissonance. It was an era of choices: composers either sought new musical forms with revolutionary experimentation or chose to apply more traditional means of expression. Musicians in the latter group—including Dohnányi—were often considered stranded in a *fin de siècle* mentality. Stravinsky, however, made an eloquent plea to close the perceived gap between old and new: "Real tradition," he declared, "is not the relic of a past that is irretrievably gone. It is a living force that animates and informs the present."

Dohnányi grew up with a strong musical awareness, developing abilities in piano, violin, organ and composition. His father, a skilled amateur cellist, cultivated friendships with some of the foremost musicians who passed through Eastern Europe, with live music-making given center stage in household activities. It was in this milieu that young Ernő developed his lifelong love of chamber music. Indeed, before his teens he publicly played Mozart's G minor Piano Quartet and wrote much chamber music. A debut solo recital came at 13, with a difficult program of Chopin, Mendelssohn, Liszt and several of his own works. At 17, already a veteran pianist and composer, he enrolled at the Royal Hungarian Academy of Music and later worked with the famous Liszt pupil Eugen d'Albert. After a widely praised and publicized graduation recital, Dohnányi—in common with Sergei Rachmaninoff five years earlier in Russia—was granted Artist's Diplomas in Piano and Composition.

As with his contemporary, the singular composer-pianist Nikolai Medtner, Dohnányi revered Beethoven, was superficially perceived under the wing of Brahms, and worked within the bounds of conventional musical forms. Though the Brahms link is especially close, Dohnányi's gifts produced an original thinker whose works stand on their own. Not only had d'Albert played both Brahms concertos under their composer's direction, but Dohnányi's composition teacher at the Academy was a great admirer and friend of the venerable composer, who enthused over Dohnányi's inspired Piano Quintet (Op. 1).

Dohnányi thus began his career with all possible advantage, armed with Brahms' endorsement and important musical connections. One of these was the great violinist Josef Joachim, who immediately recognized the young composer's gifts in conceiving and performing chamber music. Though presently considered *de rigueur* for famed pianists to perform chamber music publicly, it was a rarity at the turn of the century. Dohnányi was considered, by many contemporary accounts, among the most accomplished ensemble players of his time.

Acknowledged as a top-flight musician from the beginning, he consolidated a reputation as one of the world's most prominent pianists with triumphal solo, chamber and orchestral appearances throughout Europe, America and Russia. Critics and audiences began to speak of Dohnányi as Hungary's greatest pianist-composer since Liszt.

He was invited by Joachim to teach in Berlin, where his name's Germanic spelling, Ernst von Dohnányi, originated. While there, he composed many chamber works, as well as the *Variations on a Nursery Song* ("Twinkle, Twinkle, Little Star"), to this day his most famous work primarily because of its novelty and for instigating laughter in the concert hall. It was a joke written, he said, "for the enjoyment of fun-lovers and the annoyance of others."

After the onset of World War I, Dohnányi returned to Hungary and his alma mater (renamed the Franz Liszt Academy), and also became chief conductor of the Budapest Philharmonic Orchestra. Dohnányi left Hungary in 1918 to avoid living under the Communist dictatorship, only to return a year later as Director of the Liszt Academy. He again left briefly to protest intolerable political circumstances, then was finally dismissed after he flatly refused to fire composer Zoltán Kodály and others because of their political beliefs. The following year, though, he became president and director of the Budapest Philharmonic Society, a position from which he tirelessly championed worthy young Hungarian composers, including Bartók and Leó

Weiner. He also generously and consistently aided various charities.

The year 1928 saw Dohnányi back at the Liszt Academy, casting his considerable influence over a new generation of students including Annie Fischer, Edward Kilenyi and Georg Solti. In his *Memoirs*,* Solti remembers Dohnányi as a brilliant musician and sight-reader. This admiration was tempered by Dohnányi's habit of teaching by example—a method ill-suited to some students. He left a legacy, though, which remains strongly imprinted on new generations of Hungarian composers and pianists.

Dohnányi subsequently became music director of the Hungarian Broadcasting Society, further extending his reach as Hungary's prime musical influence. Combining roles as professor and virtuoso, he later performed an extraordinary series of ten recitals designed to provide a Baedeker of piano style through the centuries, from preclassical to then-contemporary Hungarian works. These concerts revealed a man strongly attuned to the history of musical current.

He stayed after the Nazi takeover of his country, but resigned as head of the Academy during the Second World War to protest anti-Semitic decrees as well as a demand by the Hungarian Nazi party that he fire his half-Jewish assistant. He shielded the Jewish members of his orchestra until just after Germany occupied Hungary, finally being forced to disband the group. After both of his sons were killed during the War, he had had enough, leaving for Vienna, England, Argentina and then America.

Dohnányi lacked the guile of the political animal and was actually a rather uncomplicated man with huge gifts, which he accepted naturally and without undo ego. He was, however, unshakably principled in his artistic beliefs and controlled Hungary's rich musical life with sovereign command in a turbulent era of his country's history. This stoked jealousy among some colleagues who mistook his positions and abilities as arrogance. He also estranged a crop of lesser composers by refusing to perform works he considered not up to his standards. After the war, Dohnányi became the victim of dumbfounding attacks that he was pro-Nazi, largely incited by those he alienated. His international career suffered and forced cancellations ensued. It took many years to see his reputation restored. Kilenyi, during a stint as a U.S. Army officer, was instrumental in guiding Dohnányi through the explosive post-War political climate. After an arduous immigration process, the composer ultimately settled at Florida State University in Tallahassee.

Dohnányi died at 82 while making a final series of recordings in New York City. Toward the end of his life he had resumed recording, though these later disks do not show him at his best. He disliked the sterile process of making music in a studio, always reveling in the interplay with an audience. Serious though he was toward his craft and professional obligations, Dohnányi was humorous and socially endearing; in short, here was a highly popular figure.

Dohnányi received a long series of honors and awards throughout his career, culminating with the Hungarian government's highest honor, the Kossuth Prize, bestowed thirty years after his death. Extravagantly celebrated and beloved during his lifetime, Dohnányi's posthumous descent from public awareness and favor was precipitous; he was largely written off as an historical tangent trailing Brahms' coattails. Only now has the climate changed, with today's resurgent interest in Romanticism.

The early 20th century saw the likes of Ferruccio Busoni, Rachmaninoff, Medtner and Dohnányi, musicians who could go in front of audience and orchestra, persuasively introducing their own works. In our current era of specialization, Dohnányi was among the last of this breed. Comparisons with Rachmaninoff go deeper. In addition to other endeavors, the two wrote symphonic, operatic and chamber music, and suffered from overwork and exhaustion that hastened their deaths. Each enjoyed great success playing his own Second Piano Concerto, and both had their novelty pieces: Dohnányi's *Variations on a Nursery Song* to Rachmaninoff's *Rhapsody on a Theme of Paganini*.

Rachmaninoff's music generally has more obvious melodic appeal, though Dohnányi's gifts in this regard were distinctive and are impressively on display here. Pianists will note remarkably idiomatic keyboard writing, characterizing a craftsman who knew the instrument's capabilities intimately.

Bartók and Kodály, Dohnányi's friends and fellow students at the Budapest Academy, took far greater inspiration from their country's folk music. Though the three are often referred to as the Hungarian triumvirate, Dohnányi did not generally follow their path in forging a new style based on native Hungarian rhythms and national folk songs. The cosmopolitan Dohnányi was not a stylistic groundbreaker, no matter how finely crafted and appealing his music can be. Ultimately, though, listeners and performers judge music on its visceral impact. Pianists are invited to open these pages in the spirit of inevitable discovery.

Passacaglia, Op. 6 (1899)

Here is the virtuoso as dramatist. This gothic work follows in the tradition of the Baroque's imposing organ *passacaglia*, and the glorious, chromatic keyboard works of César Franck. Dohnányi's noble contribution to the form follows the classical model of a work in continuous variation, relatively slow triple meter and harmonies generally changing with the measure. As typical in Dohnányi's music, the pianist must exercise the finest control of voicing to convey thematic transparency. In

---

*Alfred A. Knopf, New York, 1997

an unexpected *coup de théâtre*, a gorgeous rolling nocturne is introduced in E-flat major, the first of many instances in this collection employing Dohnányi's favored compositional gambit to the parallel key.

In an intriguing historical footnote, it seems likely that Dohnányi played this work for the legendary composer-pianist Leopold Godowsky shortly after its completion. They often saw each other in Budapest and America and became close friends. Godowsky undoubtedly had this piece in mind while composing his own great piano *Passacaglia* 28 years later.

Vier Rhapsodien, Op. 11 (1902–03)

The First Rhapsody, longest of the set, may be viewed as a sonata's opening movement, while the Second begins the idea of repeated musical references that each Rhapsody makes to its predecessor. A strong Hungarian quality makes this the most native of the group.

Beginning à la Prokofiev with a whimsical, spiky start, the Third Rhapsody's soaring, romantic tune, which brings Rachmaninoff to mind, made it extremely popular in its day. The concluding Rhapsody falls under the guise of the *Dies Irae* plainchant, so tellingly used by Berlioz, Liszt, Rachmaninoff and others. As if in summation, the music quotes each of its three brethren. So marks the end of this compelling set, in sweep and scope aspiring to a grand Romantic sonata.

Are the four intended to be performed together? As a group, they pose no formal key relationships and Dohnányi often programmed them separately, but their close thematic integration and overall form strongly suggest a collective presentation. Dohnányi premiered the Rhapsodies in Vienna in November 1904, the same month that saw the unveiling of Busoni's monumental Piano Concerto. The late-Romantic age was coming to a close.

Winterreigen, Op. 13 (1905)

Viktor Heindl's chimerical poem, and thus these *pasticci*, asks his friends to forget the cares of the day and lose themselves in the magic of music. Outside of the first and last of the set, each is dedicated to a friend. The poem specifically references "Schumann's dance pieces"—presumably the early *Davidsbündlertänze*. The poetry also speaks of the carnival, celebrated earlier in Schumann's *Carnaval* (Op. 9) and *Faschingsschwank aus Wien* (Op. 26). The heartfelt *Widmung*—title of Schumann's most famous song—makes this collection an homage.

Dohnányi often spoke about his music with Kilenyi, who for the present notes shared the composer's thoughts on several of these works. "My friend Victor's mazurka" presents a prankish and witty dance, transformed from one of Heindl's own compositional efforts. It is marked "Mit humor," seen often *chez* Schumann. The airborne "Music of the spheres"—referring to an ethereal sound that the Pythagoreans thought resulted from the vibration of the celestial spheres—was conceived in Vienna after its composer enjoyed a memorable flight with a balloonist friend. The graceful "Charming waltz" took its theme from a popular waltz tune of the day.

"At midnight" is an agitated chase away from trouble. Not all is serious, though, as a popular song is quoted in the bass. "Wild party" initially teeters and becomes more raucous as the evening wears on. "There were, of course, wild parties," Kilenyi acknowledged wryly. "Daybreak" finally arrives in a beautiful if sobering evocation of dawn.

After recognizing the beginning of Schumann's C major Fantasy (Op. 17), the concluding "Postlude" introduces and repeats a theme, the first three notes of which spell *A-d-e*, the German word for "farewell." Schumann's music, at times light-hearted and ironic, regularly touched the more serious elements of passion and pathos. Dohnányi's fluent treatment of Schumannesque style, along with his faith in Heindl's words, gives the *Winter Rounds* their distinction.

Humoresken in Form einer Suite, Op. 17 (1907)

Schumann's own *Humoreske* (Op. 20), filled with irony and extreme emotional contrasts, reflects his understanding of *Humor* and gives context to Dohnányi's suite. The four ancient Greek humors—the Melancholy, the Sanguine, the Phlegmatic and the Choleric—are touched upon in a youthful way, while the centuries-old names given to each piece engender a further sense of looking back in time. Dohnányi's enthusiasm for baroque dance forms may also be seen in his *Suite in the Olden Style* (Op. 24) and in the early *Gavotte and Musette*. The Toccata of Op. 17 reveals its debt to Bach in name and feel. Its middle section (p. 124) paraphrases the virtuosic second Prelude from *The Well-Tempered Clavier* in the same C minor key.

One of Dohnányi's favorite forms was Theme with Variations. The Pavane from the 16th Century with Variations alludes to that century's Italian court dances. The middle *scherzando* opens with a Latin phrase, "We are young, therefore we rejoice." The Pastorale borrows another 16th-century term, used to describe a dramatic performance with an idyllic plot, typically written in a moderate 6/8 meter. The Introduction and Fugue serves as a substantial conclusion to the Suite. Dohnányi's frequent choice of key signatures employing many flats and sharps, as here, further extends the range of harmonic possibilities and often brings him squarely into the 20th century.

Sechs Konzertetüden, Op. 28 (1916)

Brain and fingers operate in concert to dominate the elaborate complexity of these pieces. The First Etude is an animated study recalling Mendelssohn's Op. 104, No. 3, and sharing the same A minor key. The kittenish Second Etude gives equal weight to developing the right and left hands in a capricious chase to the end. Its inspiration was Chopin's Etude, Op. 25, No. 8, in the same key. The E-flat minor Etude is a whirlwind, with interlocking notes granting it a vertiginous attitude. Liszt's intricate study in interlaced notes, the Paganini Etude No. 4, is but a warm-up next to this piece.

Liszt appears once again, as the B-flat minor Etude recalls a debt to his Transcendental Etude No. 7, "Eroica," which Dohnányi studied with d'Albert. As a kaleidoscopic *moto perpetuo,* the Fifth Etude parallels those by Godowsky and Weber. The Mendelssohnian Capriccio in F Minor is the best known of the set, frequently performed by Rachmaninoff, Godowsky, Horowitz and many great virtuosi.

Dohnányi rarely allotted much practice to his own compositions, feeling that with all the time spent on their conception, they would lose freshness with overwork. He was thus not the ideal performer of his own music. As a group, then, the lapidary brilliance of these chiseled Etudes remains to be heard to full effect.

Variationen über ein ungarisches Volkslied, Op. 29 (1917)

Haydn and Schubert, among other composers, made use of Hungarian folk tunes in their music. Brahms based his perennially-performed Hungarian Dances on popular Magyar melodies played by Gypsies he heard, and loosely quoted this style in other compositions. Liszt paid his own tribute in the freely adapted Hungarian Rhapsodies.

Composed during the First World War, this archetype was Dohnányi's first effort based entirely on a traditional Hungarian folk song. Yearning and doleful, its frequent *rubato* indications recall how freely the Gypsies treated their ancient tunes.

Pastorale: "Mennyből az angyal" (1920)

Adapted from the traditional Hungarian Christmas carol "Mennyből az angyal" ("The angel is from heaven"), this idyllic work was premiered in Budapest, at Christmastime 1920. Here, the meaning of "pastorale" differs from that seen in the fourth Humoresque. The name derives from pieces imitating the shawms and pipes of biblical shepherds at the birth of Jesus. A *pastorale* thus came to assume the nature of peaceful Christmas music, examples of which may be found in Bach, Handel, Beethoven and others. Dohnányi considered his luminous Pastorale a memorable recital and encore piece. Its quietly ecstatic bearing finds spiritual kinship with Shostakovich's later Preludes and Fugues (Op. 87).

Countless works of Beethoven and Chopin may still sound appealing with less than inspired performances; figures as diverse as Gabriel Fauré, Alexander Scriabin, Medtner and Dohnányi, however, wrote music that simply falls flat with cautious, safe interpretations. Pianists accepting the challenges of Dohnányi's music need not see themselves as vendors of the arcane. This vital body of work awaits its true representation on recordings and in the concert hall.

Robert Rimm
Philadelphia, 1999

ROBERT RIMM, managing partner of Chronos Studios in Philadelphia, combines the disciplines of music and language as educator, pianist, writer and translator. He is author of an anthology of 19th- and 20th-century pianist/composers and his articles regularly appear in prominent music publications. Mr. Rimm is a graduate of the University of Pennsylvania.

Dedicated to Mrs. Oliverson, in friendship

Passacaglia
Op. 6 (1899)

Passacaglia (Op. 6)

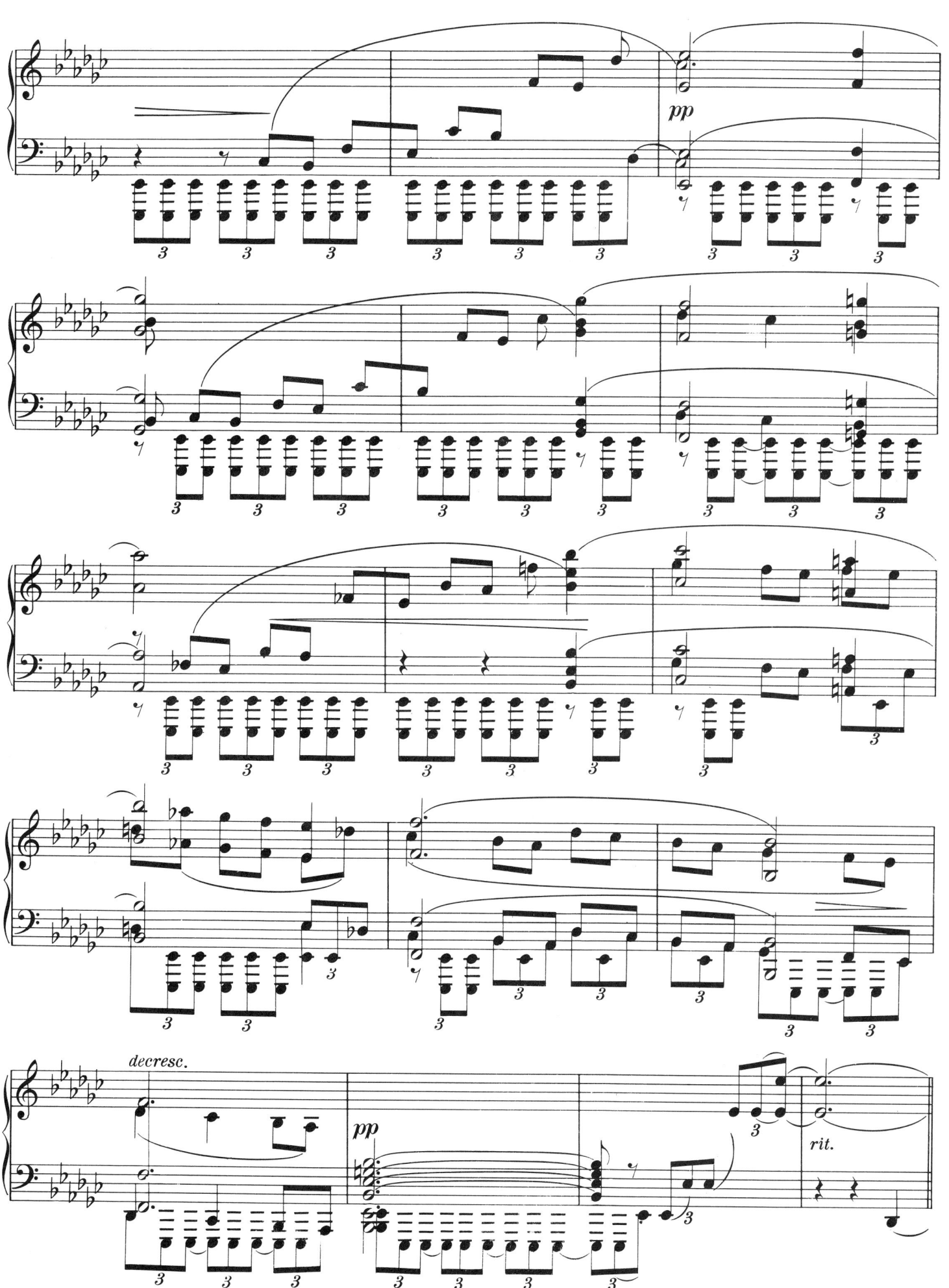

Passacaglia (Op. 6)

4 *Passacaglia* (Op. 6)

Passacaglia (Op. 6)

Passacaglia (Op. 6)

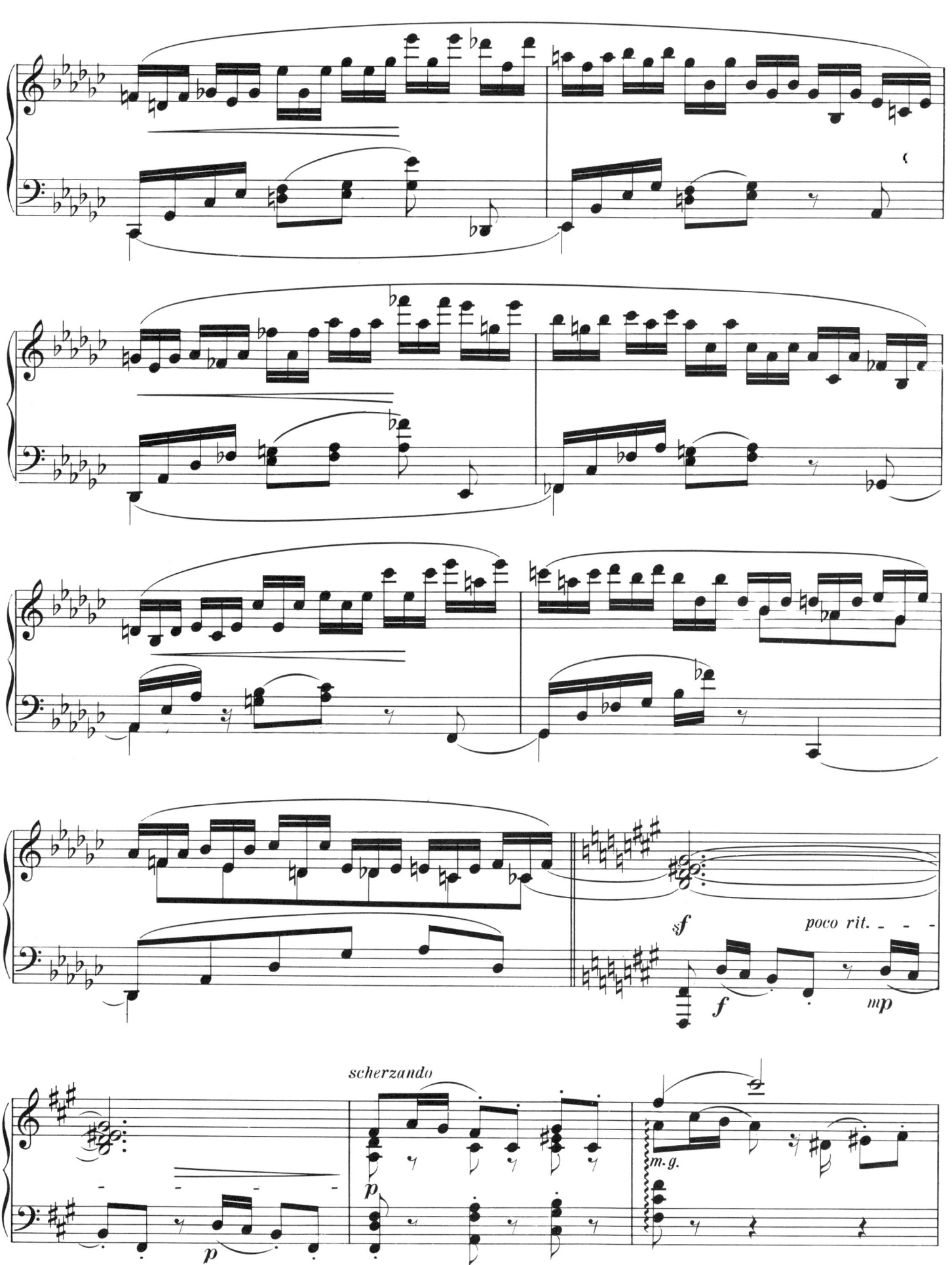

Passacaglia (Op. 6)

8 *Passacaglia* (Op. 6)

Passacaglia (Op. 6)

Passacaglia (Op. 6)

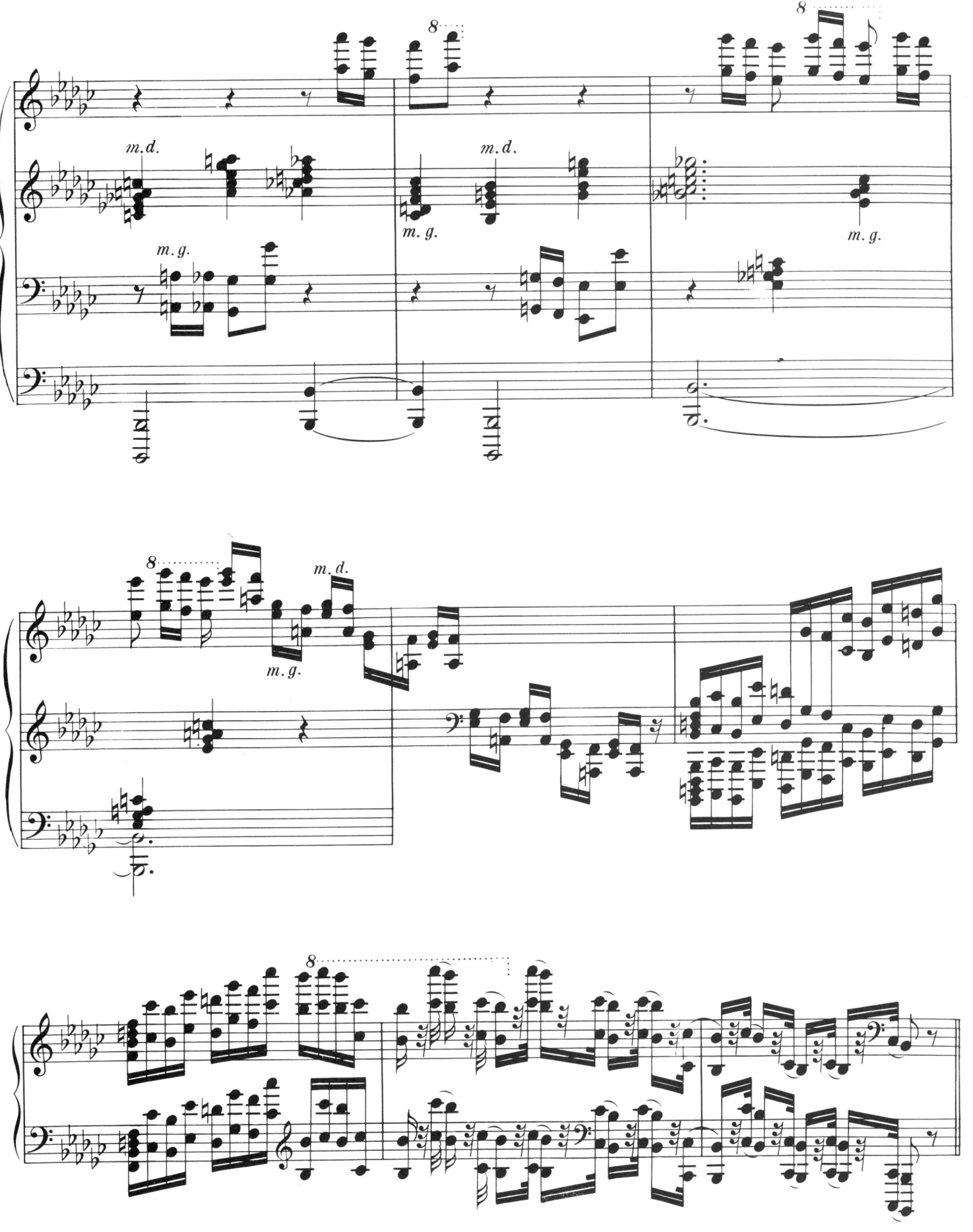

Passacaglia (Op. 6)

12 *Passacaglia* (Op. 6)

Passacaglia (Op. 6)

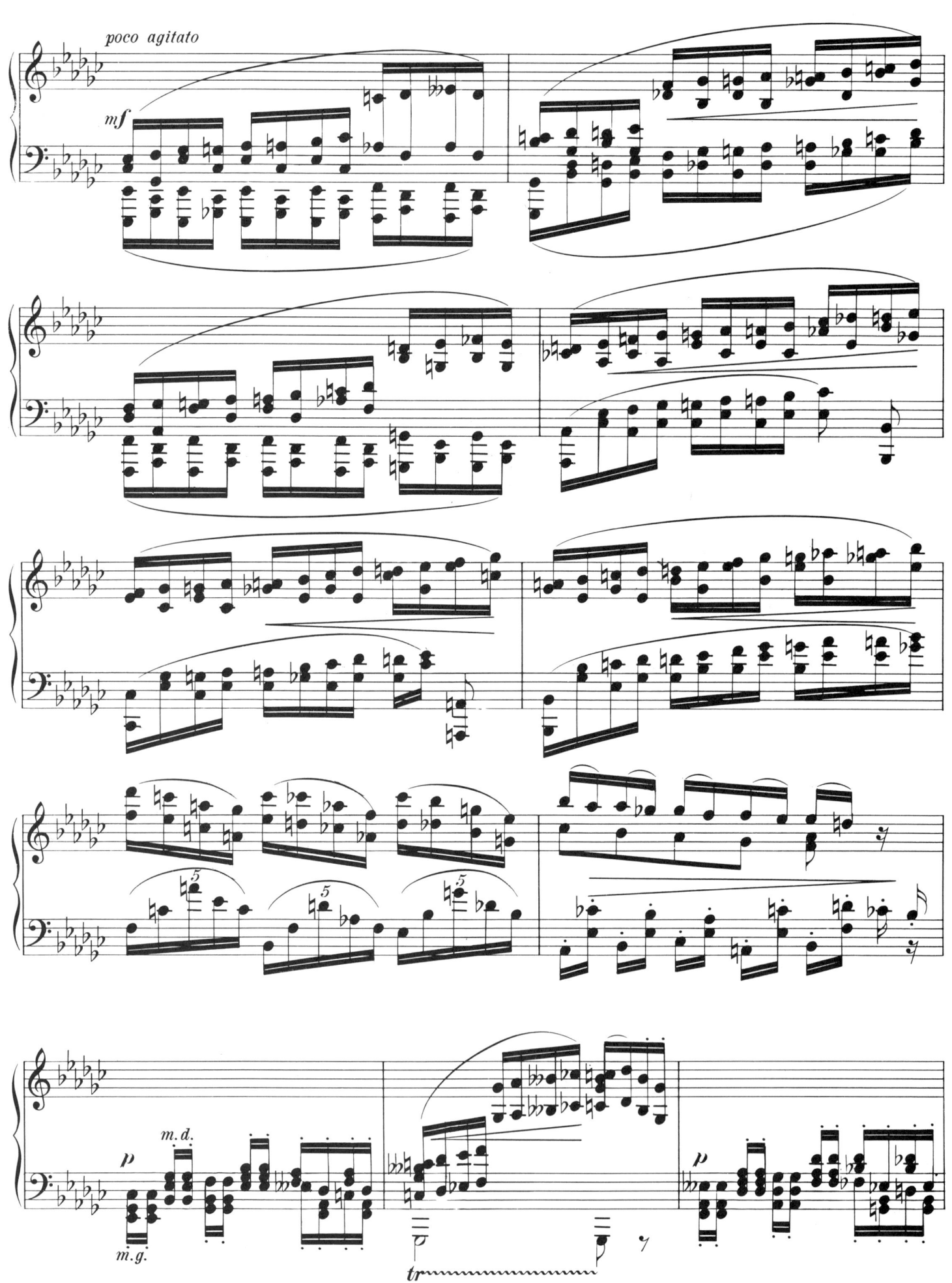

14 *Passacaglia* (Op. 6)

Passacaglia (Op. 6)

Passacaglia (Op. 6)

Passacaglia (Op. 6)

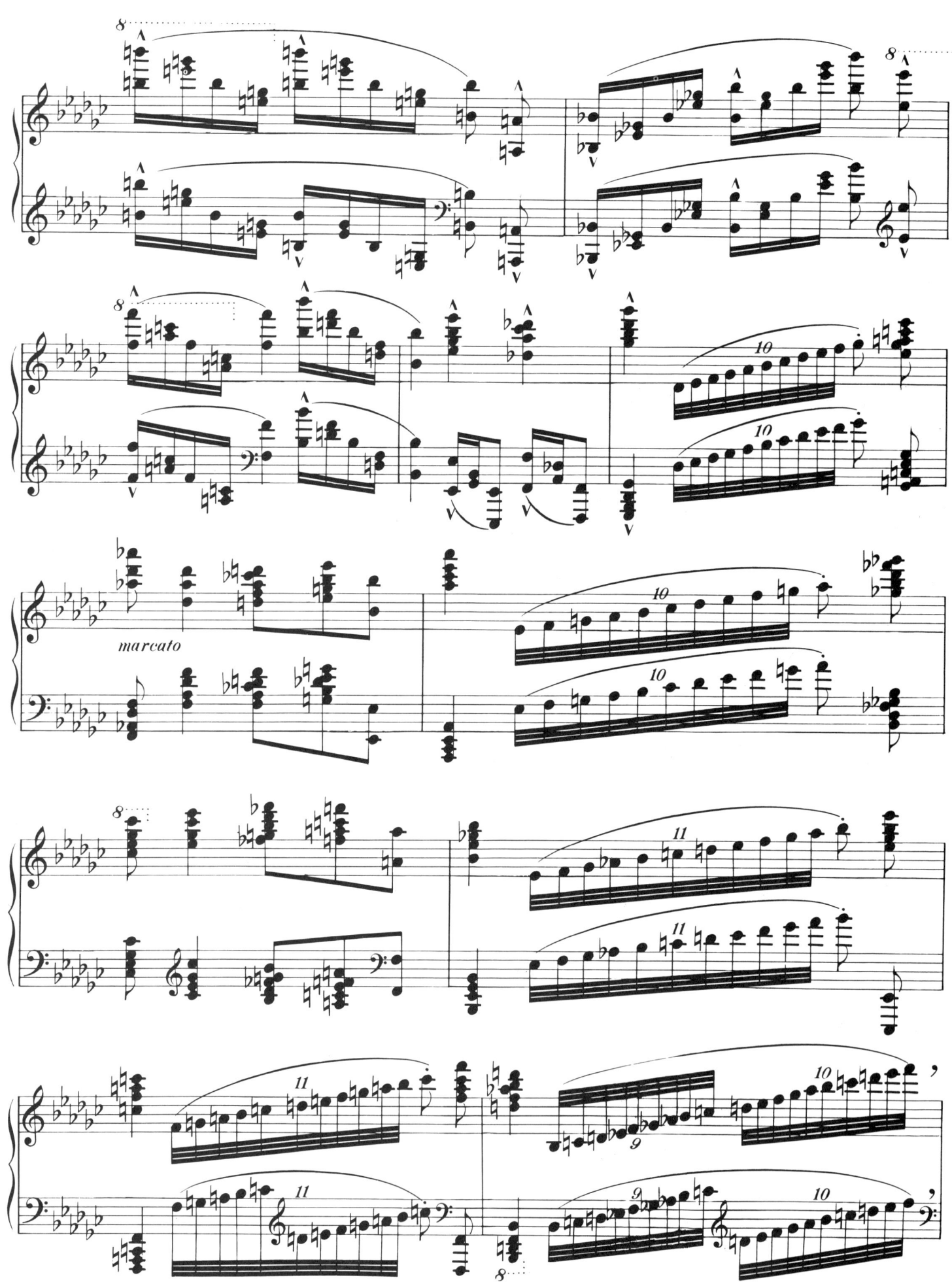

18 *Passacaglia* (Op. 6)

Passacaglia (Op. 6)

20 *Passacaglia* (Op. 6)

Passacaglia (Op. 6)

22 *Passacaglia* (Op. 6)

Passacaglia (Op. 6)

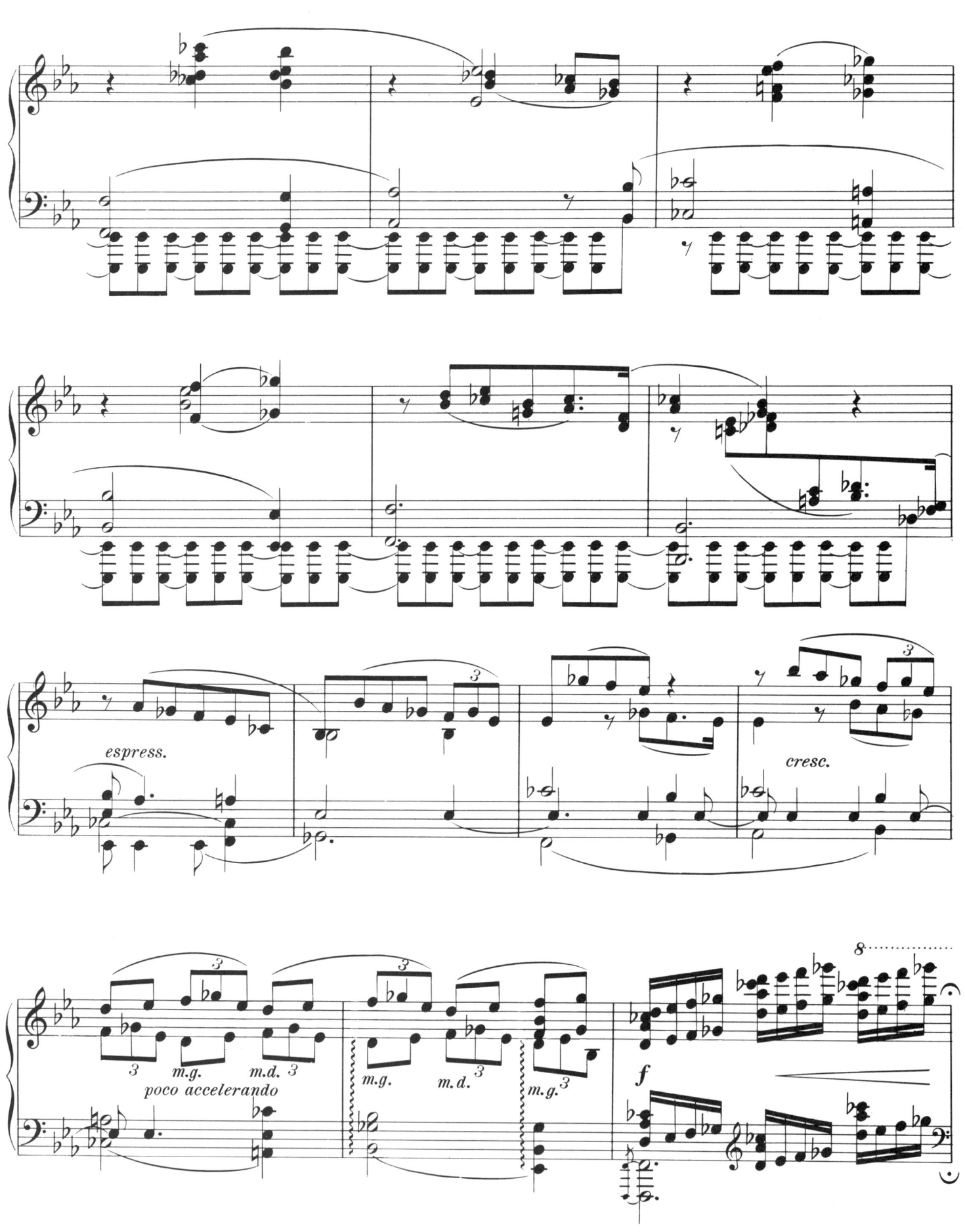

Passacaglia (Op. 6)

Passacaglia (Op. 6)

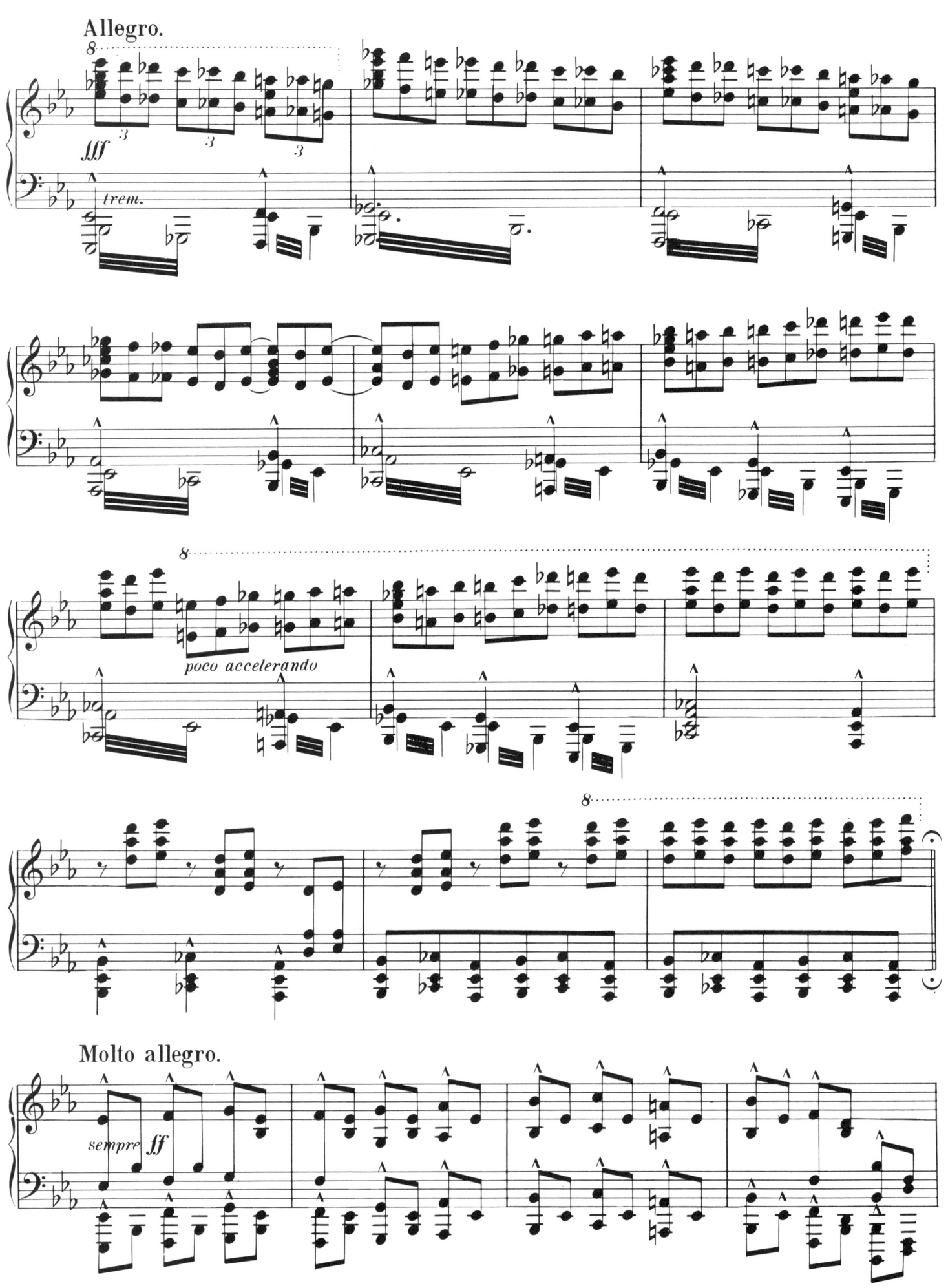

Passacaglia (Op. 6)

Passacaglia (Op. 6)

To his friend Prof. Stephan Thomán

VIER RHAPSODIEN
Four Rhapsodies
Op. 11 (1902–3)

Rhapsody No. 1 in G Minor

Four Rhapsodies (Op. 11)

Four Rhapsodies (Op. 11)

*The meaning of this "ad lib." is that, if desired, the octaves may also be played several times *crescendo* and *decrescendo* in free tempo. The same holds for similar "ad lib." passages as well.

32   Four Rhapsodies (Op. 11)

Four Rhapsodies (Op. 11)

34   Four Rhapsodies (Op. 11)

Four Rhapsodies (Op. 11)

36 Four Rhapsodies (Op. 11)

38 *Four Rhapsodies* (Op. 11)

Four Rhapsodies (Op. 11)

Four Rhapsodies (Op. 11)

42 *Four Rhapsodies* (Op. 11)

Rhapsody No. 2 in F-sharp Minor
From Op. 11 (1902–3)

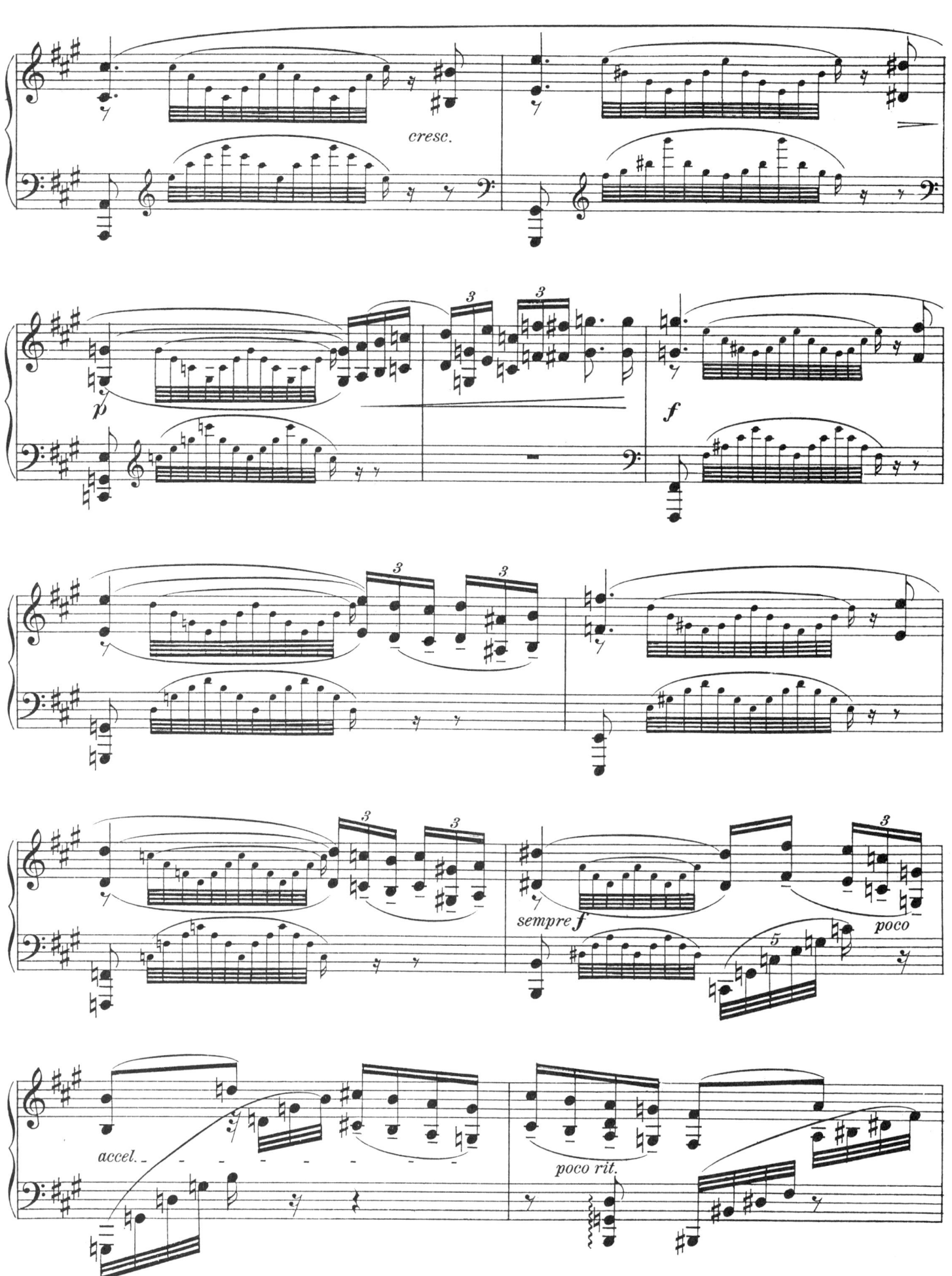

Four Rhapsodies (Op. 11)

Four Rhapsodies (Op. 11)

50 *Four Rhapsodies* (Op. 11)

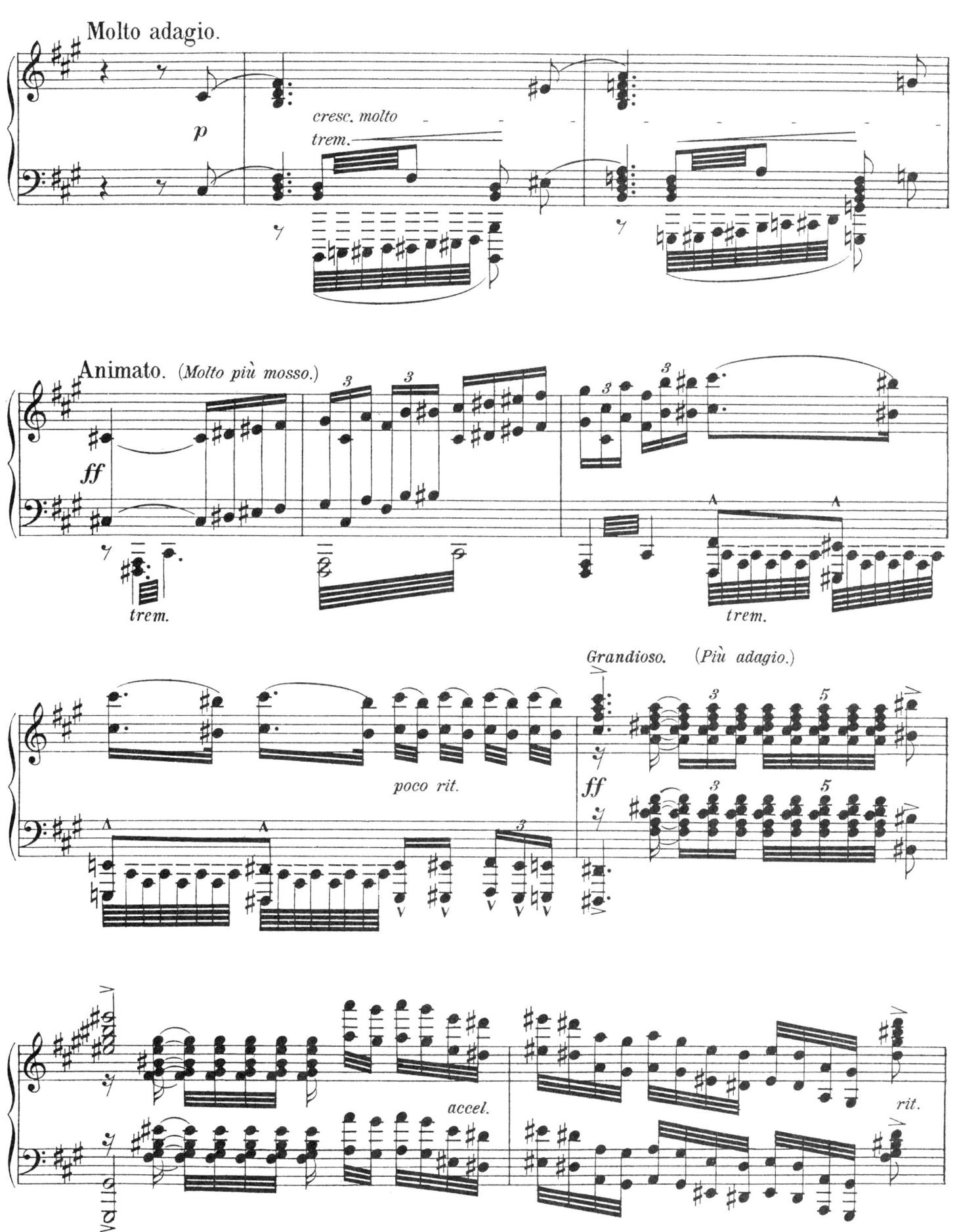

Four Rhapsodies (Op. 11)

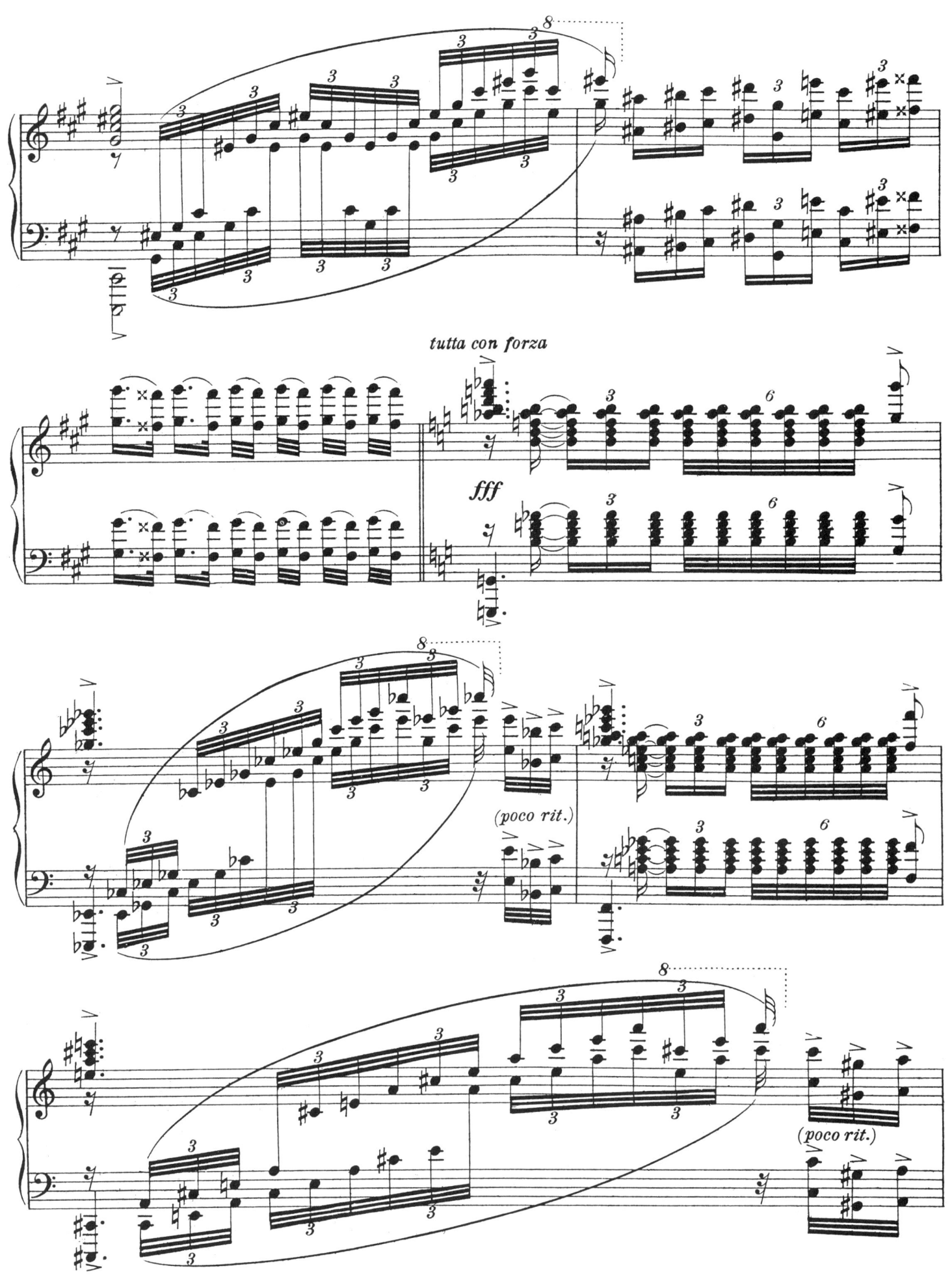

52 *Four Rhapsodies* (Op. 11)

54 *Four Rhapsodies* (Op. 11)

Four Rhapsodies (Op. 11)

Rhapsody No. 3 in C Major

From Op. 11 (1902–3)

Four Rhapsodies (Op. 11)

Four Rhapsodies (Op. 11)

Four Rhapsodies (Op. 11)

Four Rhapsodies (Op. 11)

Four Rhapsodies (Op. 11)

62 *Four Rhapsodies* (Op. 11)

Four Rhapsodies (Op. 11)

64   *Four Rhapsodies* (Op. 11)

Four Rhapsodies (Op. 11)

66　*Four Rhapsodies* (Op. 11)

Rhapsody No. 4 in E-flat Minor
From Op. 11 (1902–3)

Four Rhapsodies (Op. 11)

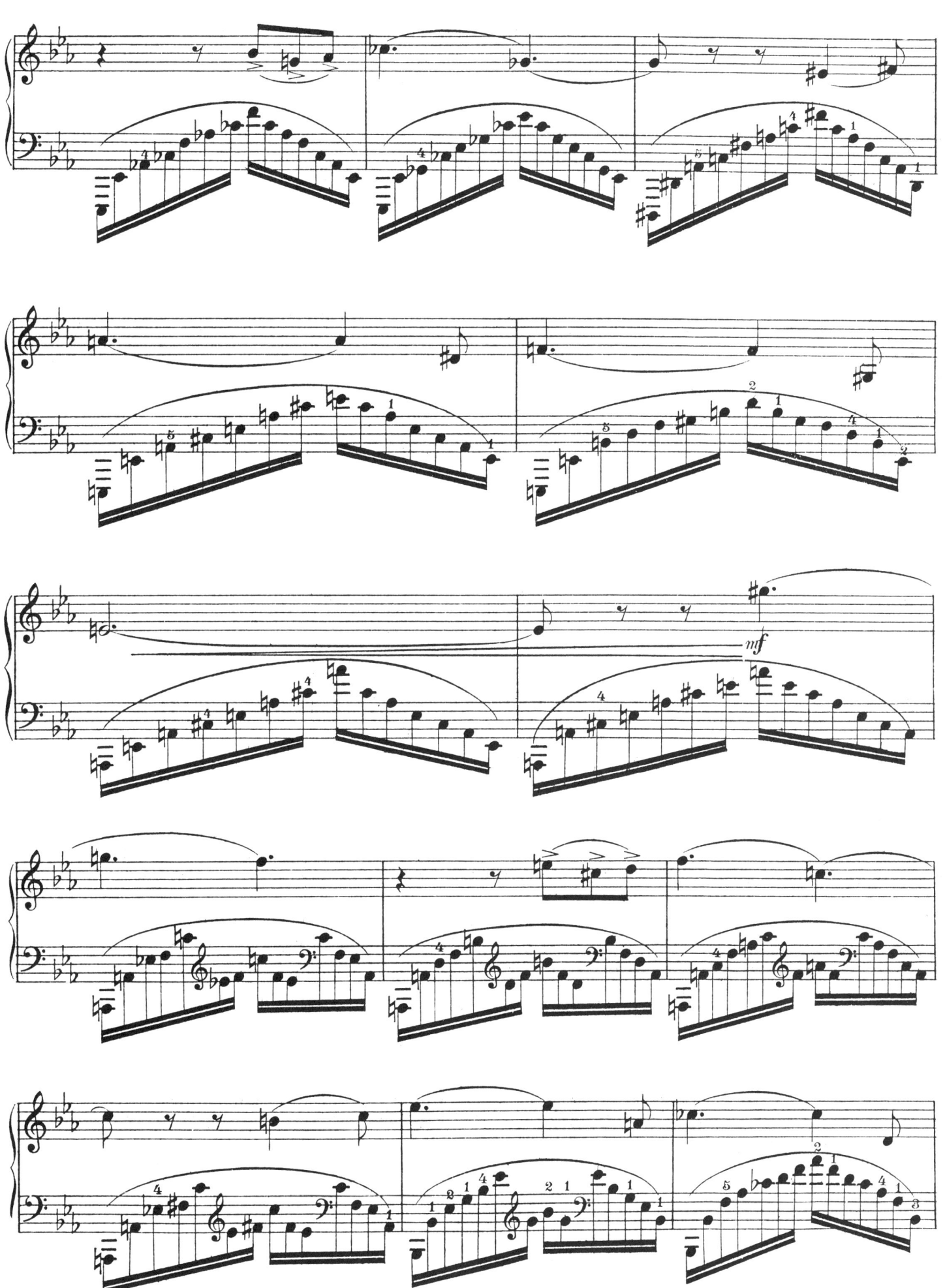

Four Rhapsodies (Op. 11)

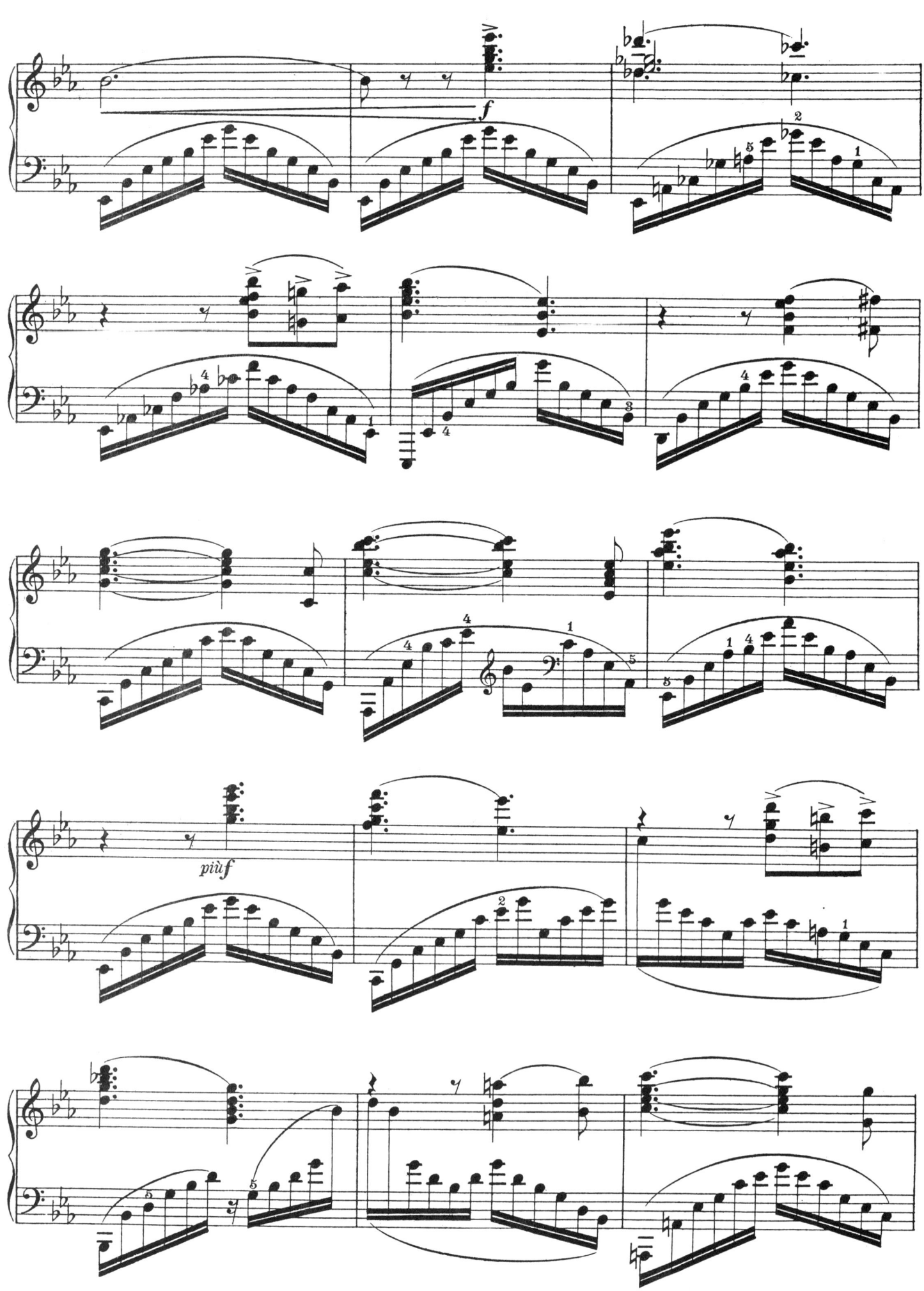

Four Rhapsodies (Op. 11)

Four Rhapsodies (Op. 11)

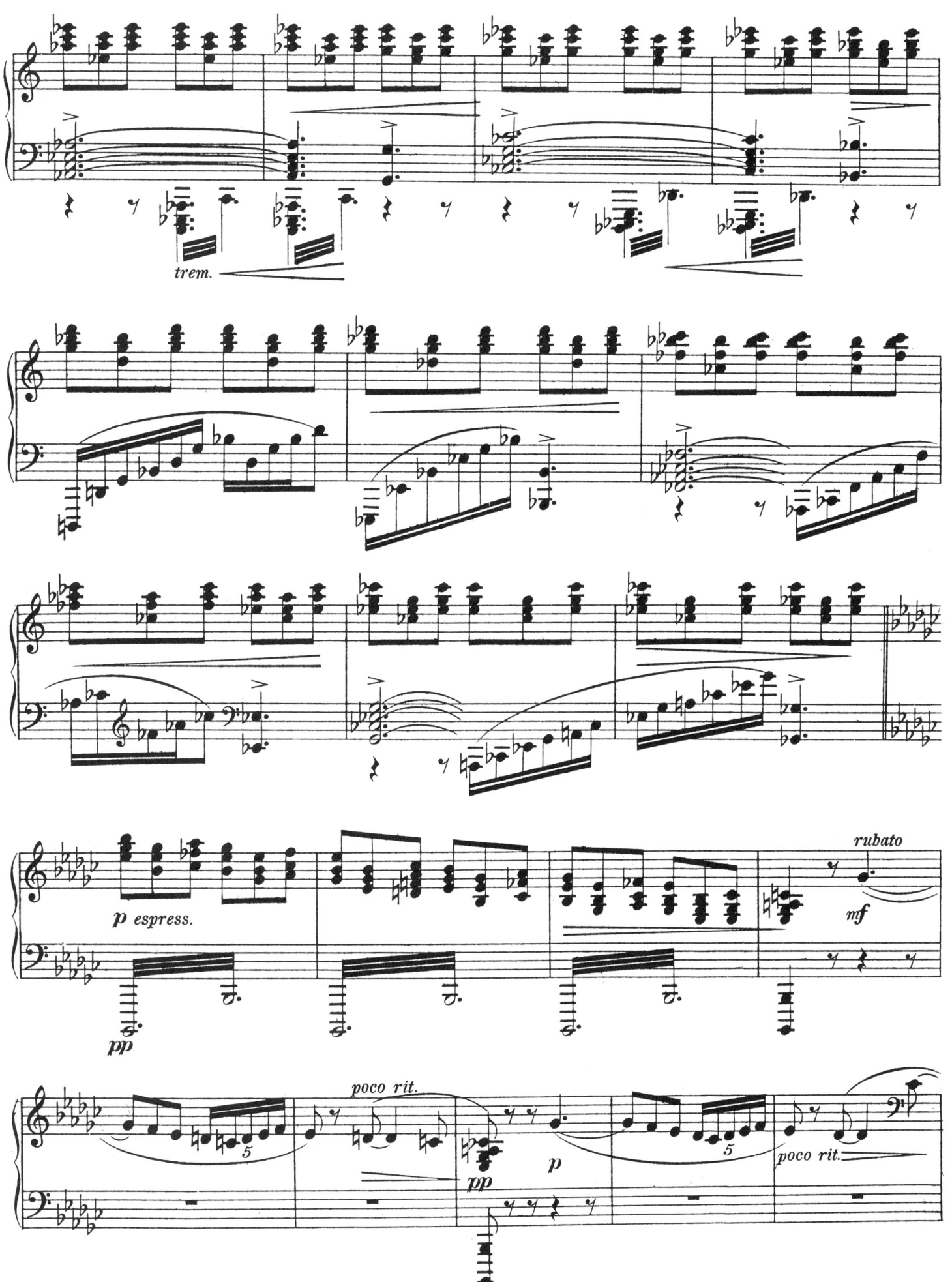

Four Rhapsodies (Op. 11)

74 *Four Rhapsodies* (Op. 11)

Four Rhapsodies (Op. 11)

76 *Four Rhapsodies* (Op. 11)

WINTERREIGEN
Winter Rounds: 10 Bagatelles
Op. 13 (1905)

Widmung
Dedication (Op. 13, No. 1)

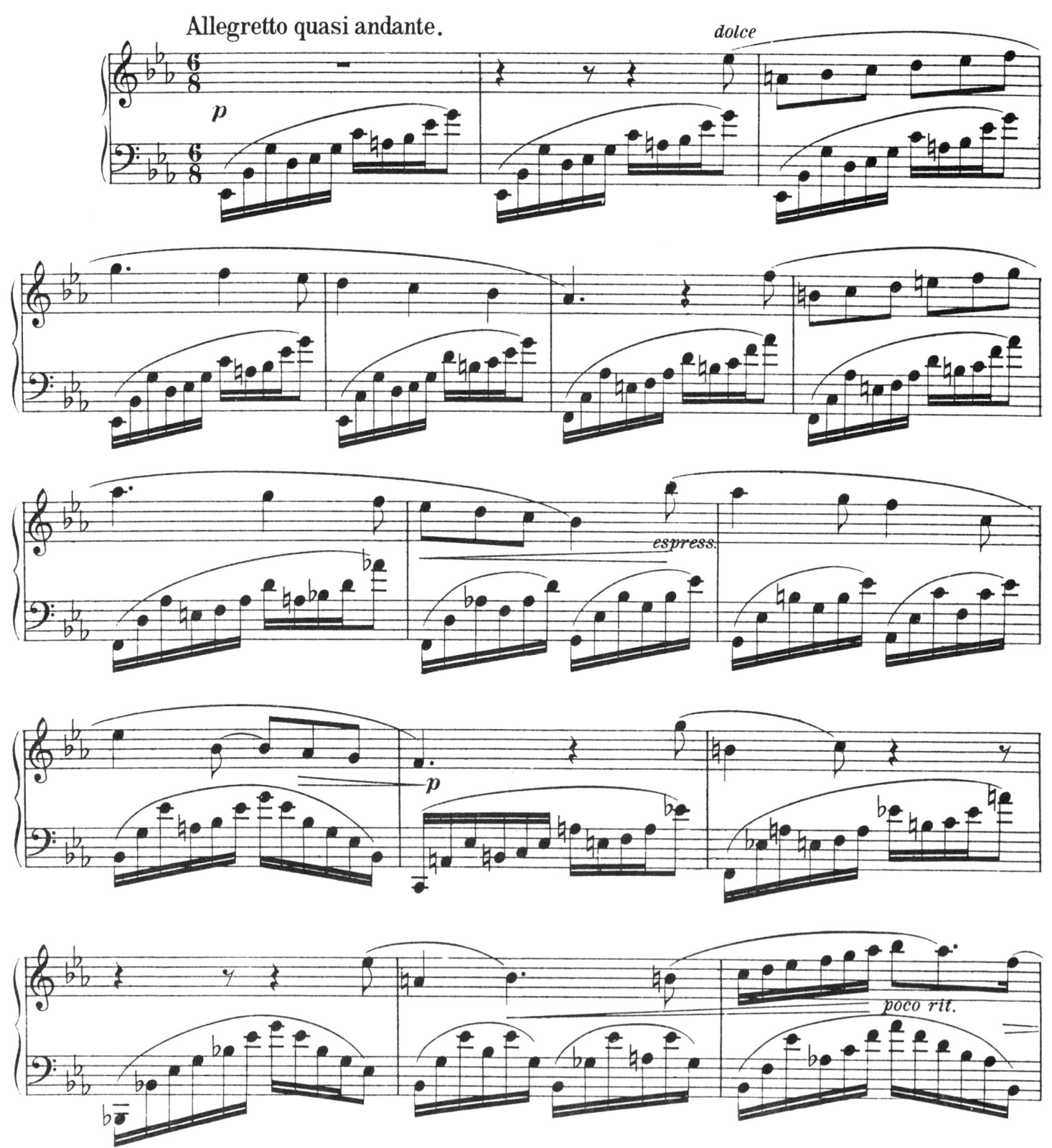

Winter Rounds (Op. 13)

To my friend Bob

Marsch der lustigen Brüder
March of the merry companions (Op. 13, No. 2)

Winter Rounds (Op. 13)   81

Winter Rounds (Op. 13)

Winter Rounds (Op. 13)

An Ada

To Ada (Op. 13, No. 3)

Freund Victor's Mazurka

My friend Victor's mazurka (Op. 13, No. 4)

86 *Winter Rounds* (Op. 13)

Winter Rounds (Op. 13)

88 Winter Rounds (Op. 13)

Winter Rounds (Op. 13)

To my friend Korwin

Sphärenmusik
Music of the spheres (Op. 13, No. 5)

Adagio ma non troppo.

Winter Rounds (Op. 13)

92 Winter Rounds (Op. 13)

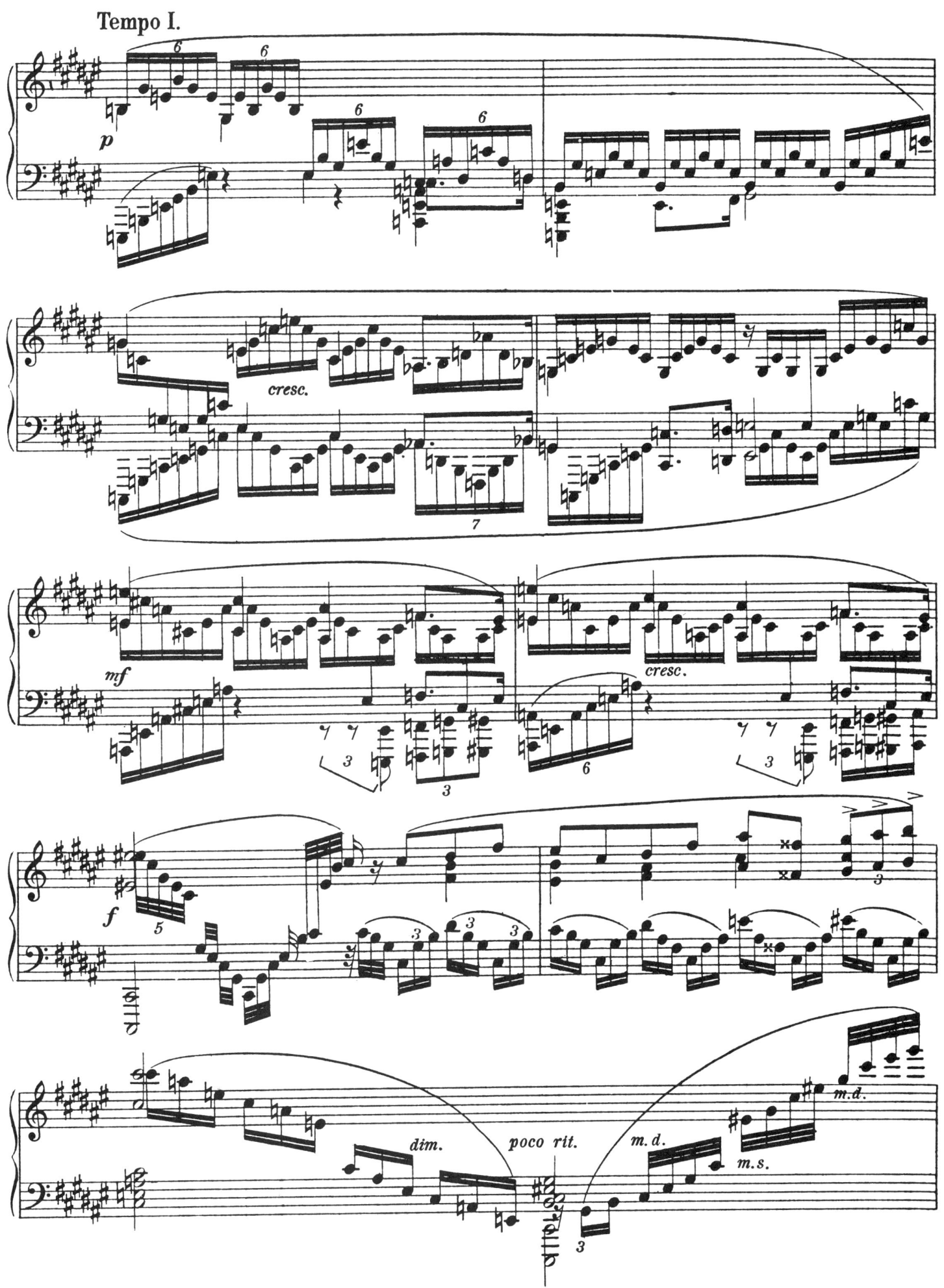

94 Winter Rounds (Op. 13)

Winter Rounds (Op. 13)

96 *Winter Rounds* (Op. 13)

To my friend Jan

Valse aimable
Charming waltz (Op. 13, No. 6)

Winter Rounds (Op. 13)

98   Winter Rounds (Op. 13)

Winter Rounds (Op. 13)

To my friend Aujust

Um Mitternacht
At midnight (Op. 13, No. 7)

100 *Winter Rounds* (Op. 13)

Winter Rounds (Op. 13)

Winter Rounds (Op. 13)

To my friend Naz

Tolle Gesellschaft
Wild party (Op. 13, No. 8)

104 *Winter Rounds* (Op. 13)

Winter Rounds (Op. 13)

Winter Rounds (Op. 13)

Winter Rounds (Op. 13)

108 *Winter Rounds* (Op. 13)

Winter Rounds (Op. 13)

To my friend Lindner

Morgengrauen
Daybreak (Op. 13, No. 9)

Winter Rounds (Op. 13)

Postludium

(Op. 13, No. 10)

Allegro non troppo.

112 *Winter Rounds* (Op. 13)

Winter Rounds (Op. 13) 113

WINTERREIGEN

Nun laßt, o laßt des Tages Sorgen schweigen,
Die Sternennacht lauscht draußen klar und kalt,
Und in der Töne Zauberbanngewalt
Laßt uns das Ohr nach fernen Träumen neigen!

In der Erinnerung Gold getaucht
Ersteht in neuem Glanz, ihr Festtagsstunden,
Da Frohsinnslaune rasch zerblies manch' Sorgenschleier,
Der uns des Daseins Freude grämend überhüllt!
Ersteh' in neuem Glanz, du frohe Stadt am Donauufer,
Ein feingetönter, jubelnder Akkord! — —
Ihr Freunde, rasch reicht Euch die Hand zu tollem Fastnachtsreigen!
Ihr bangen Warner, scheltet nicht:
Wer edel denkt, macht Edles stets sich allerorts zu eigen.
Welch schöner Märchentraum!
Enteilet nicht, ihr wirbelbunten Bilder!—
Ha! schäumst du wieder, sinnberauschend duft'ger Trank?
Nehmt, Freunde, hin, ich will das Beste heute mit Euch teilen,
Ein lebenswarmes Stück der Jugend, der Erinnerung! — — —
Welch leiser Ton winkt mir zu Ende?
„Ade"? — — — — — — — — — — — — — —

Es blättert meine Freundin sinnend lauschend am Klavier
— — — — — Aus einem Band von Schumanns Reigenwerken
Fiel einer nächtig dunkelroten Rose
Welkes Blatt — — — — —

Viktor Heindl

WINTER ROUNDS

Now let, oh let the day's cares be silent,
The starry night outside is listening, clear and cold,
And in the magic spell of the music's might
Let us incline our ear to faraway dreams!

Immersed in the gold of memory,
Be revived in new splendor, you holiday hours,
When a happy mood quickly dispelled many a mist of cares
That grimly overshadowed the joy of our existence!
Be revived in new splendor, you joyful city on the banks of the Danube,
In a fine-tuned jubilant harmony! — —
Friends, quickly take one another's hand for a madcap Carnival round!
You timid counselors, do not find fault with us:
A man with a noble mind makes noble things his own always and everywhere.
What a beautiful fairy-tale dream!
Do not rush away, you colorful, spinning images!—
Ha! Are you foaming again, you fragrant, intoxicating brew?
Take this, friends, I want to share the best with you today,
A slice of youth and memory warm with life! — — —
What quiet sound beckons to me at the end?
"Farewell"? — — — — — — — — — — — — —

My lady friend, musing and listening at the piano, is leafing through an album
— — — — — Out of a volume of Schumann's dance pieces
Fell a withered petal
From a rose of a red as dark as night. — — — — —

English translation by Stanley Appelbaum

HUMORESKEN IN FORM EINER SUITE
Humoresques in the form of a suite
Op. 17 (1907)

Marsch
March (Op. 17, No. 1)

Humoresques (Op. 17)

Humoresques (Op. 17)

Humoresques (Op. 17)

Toccata
(Op. 17, No. 2)

Allegro molto.

122 *Humoresques* (Op. 17)

Humoresques (Op. 17)

124 *Humoresques* (Op. 17)

Humoresques (Op. 17)

Humoresques (Op. 17)

Humoresques (Op. 17)

Pavane
aus dem 16. Jahrhundert mit Variationem
Pavane from the 16th century with variations
(Op. 17, No. 3)

Humoresques (Op. 17)

136 *Humoresques* (Op. 17)

Humoresques (Op. 17)

Var. 5.
Tranquillo (Tempo I.)

138 *Humoresques* (Op. 17)

Humoresques (Op. 17)

Pastorale
(Op. 17, No. 4)

Humoresques (Op. 17)

Humoresques (Op. 17)

Humoresques (Op. 17)

144 *Humoresques* (Op. 17)

Humoresques (Op. 17) 145

Introduction und Fuge
Introduction and fugue (Op. 17, No. 5)

Humoresques (Op. 17)

NB: Each time the trill should be executed as a quintuplet:

Humoresques (Op. 17)

Humoresques (Op. 17)

NB: Simplification for small hands:

152   *Humoresques* (Op. 17)

Humoresques (Op. 17)

154   *Humoresques* (Op. 17)

Humoresques (Op. 17)

Humoresques (Op. 17)

Humoresques (Op. 17)

SECHS KONZERTETÜDEN
Six concert etudes
Op. 28 (1916)

Etude No. 1 in A Minor

Six Etudes (Op. 28)

162   *Six Etudes* (Op. 28)

Six Etudes (Op. 28)

164 *Six Etudes* (Op. 28)

Six Etudes (Op. 28)

Etude No. 2 in D-flat Major
From Op. 28 (1916)

Six Etudes (Op. 28)

Etude No. 3 in E-flat Minor
From Op. 28 (1916)

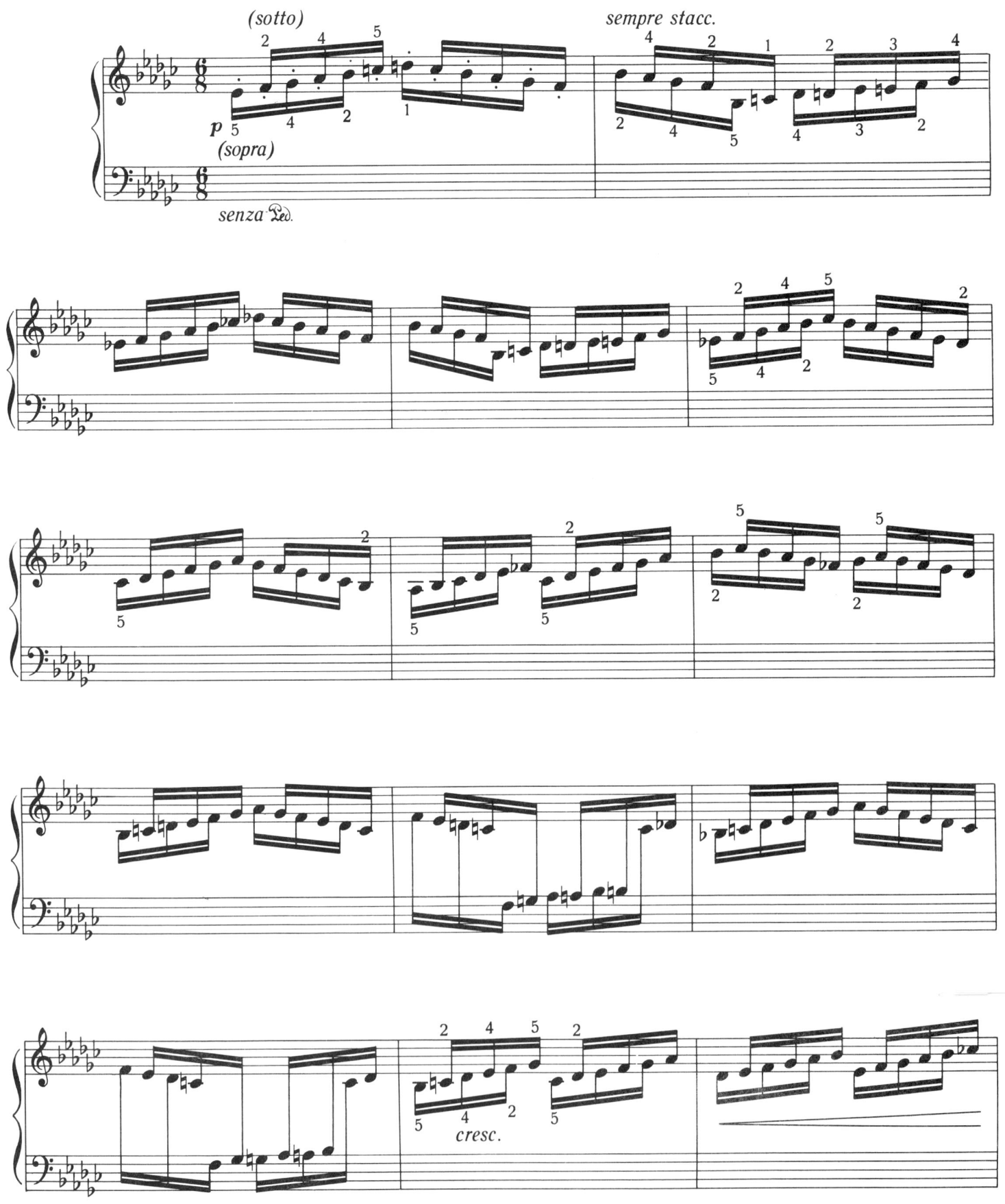

Six Etudes (Op. 28)

Six Etudes (Op. 28)

Six Etudes (Op. 28)

174 *Six Etudes* (Op. 28)

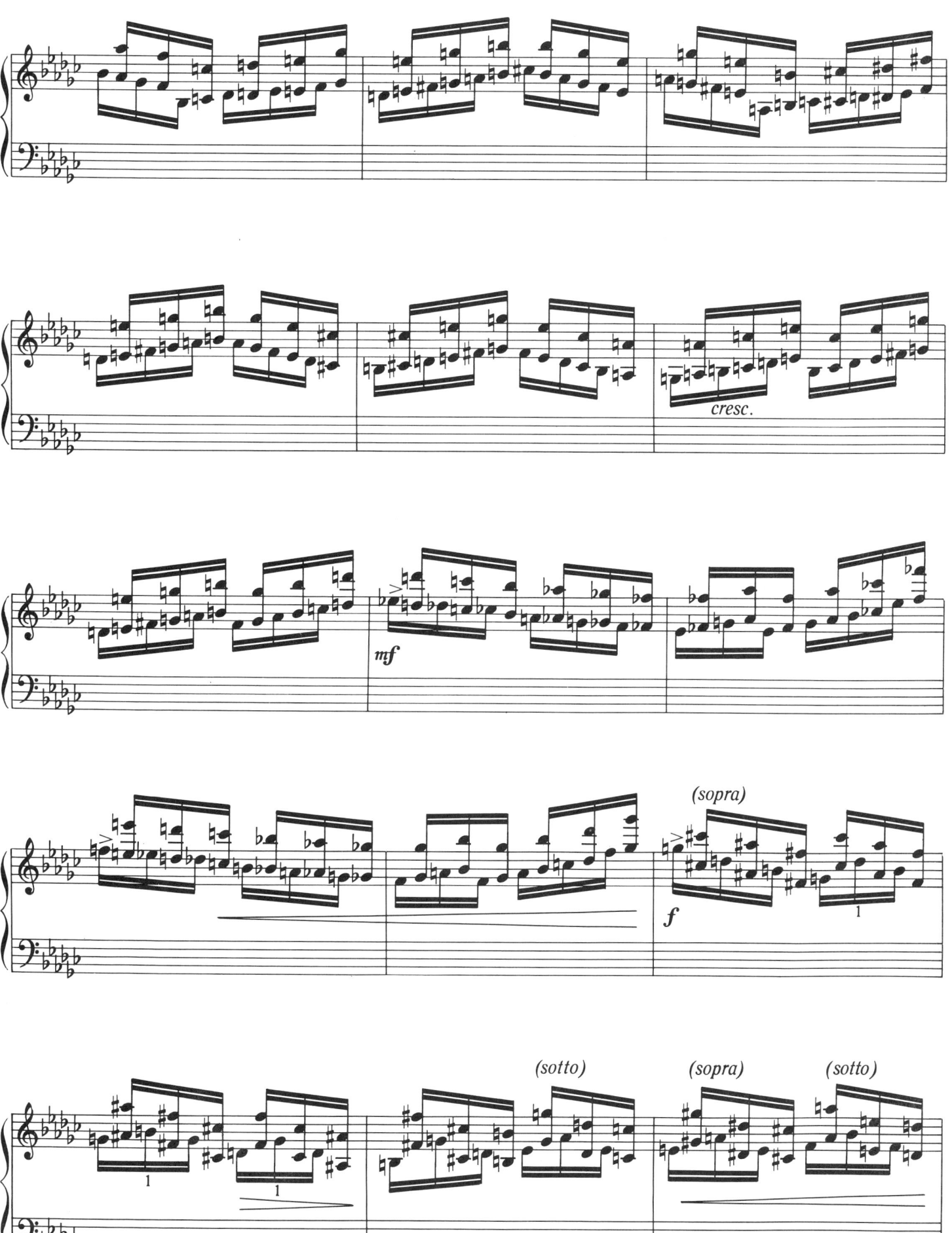

Six Etudes (Op. 28)

Six Etudes (Op. 28)

Six Etudes (Op. 28)

178 *Six Etudes* (Op. 28)

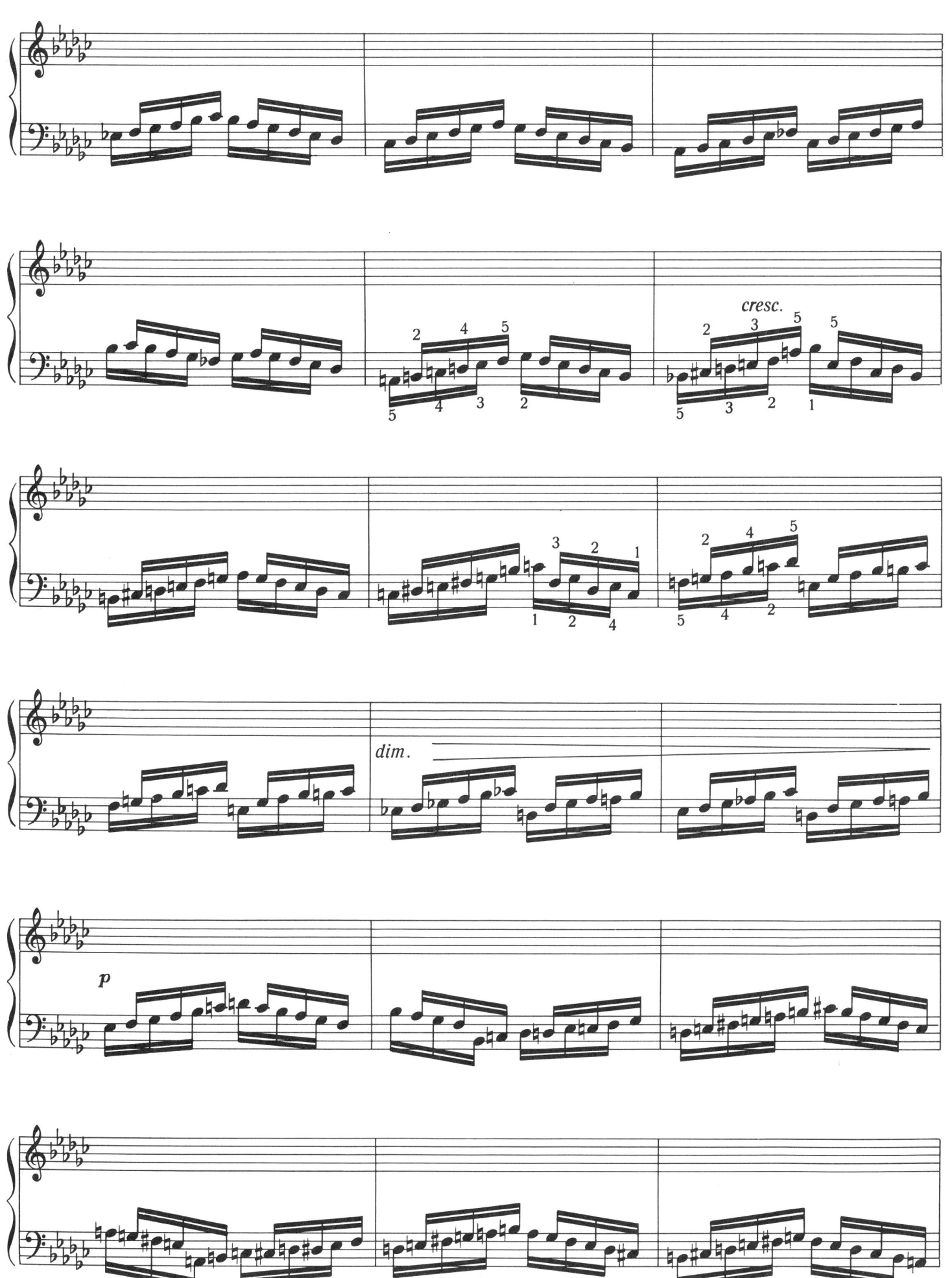

Six Etudes (Op. 28)

Etude No. 4 in B-flat Minor
From Op. 28 (1916)

Six Etudes (Op. 28)

184 *Six Etudes* (Op. 28)

Six Etudes (Op. 28)

Six Etudes (Op. 28)

Six Etudes (Op. 28)

Etude No. 5 in E Major
From Op. 28 (1916)

NB: Left hand plays the downstemmed notes; right hand plays the upstemmed notes.

Six Etudes (Op. 28)

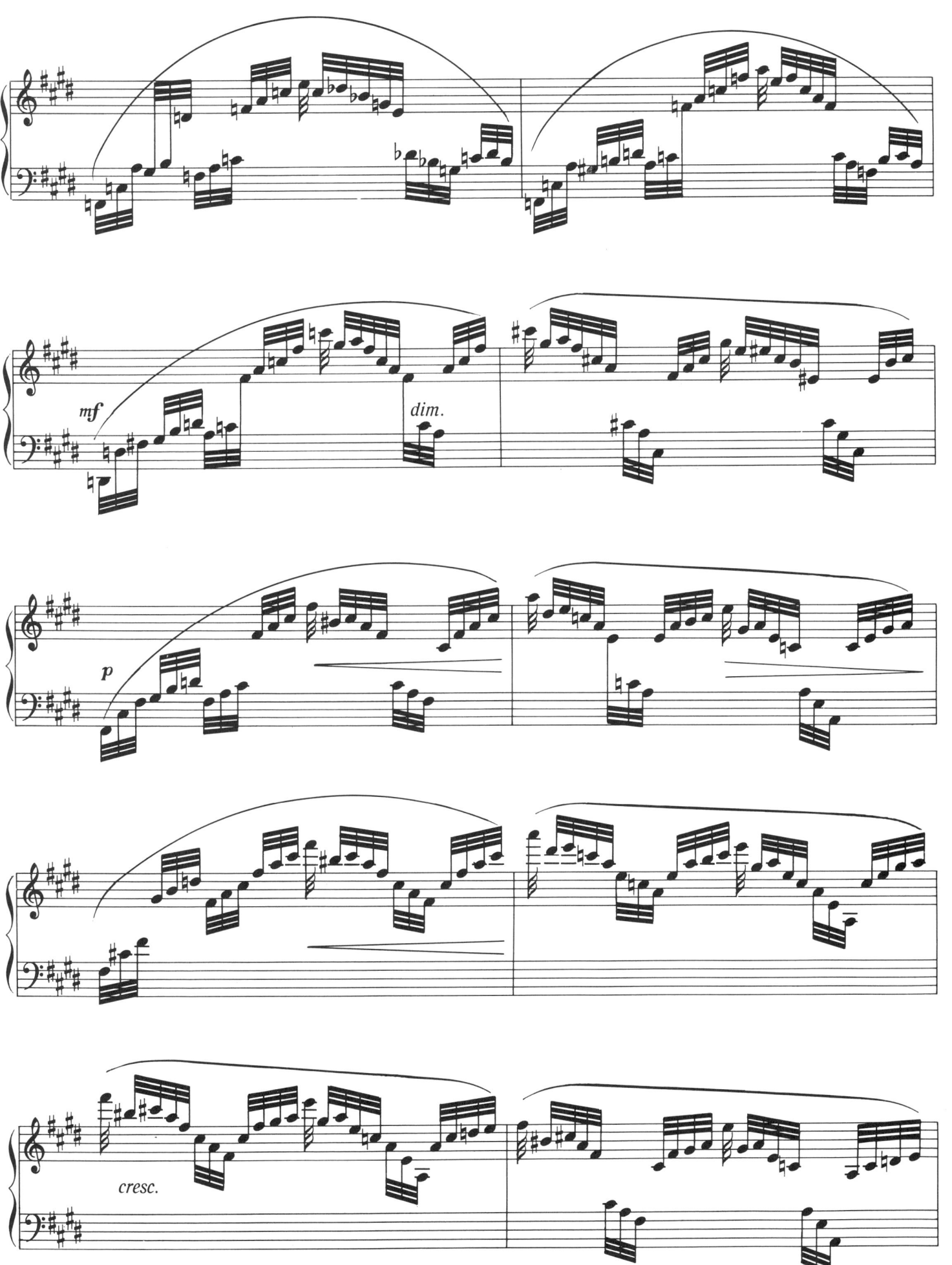

Six Etudes (Op. 28)

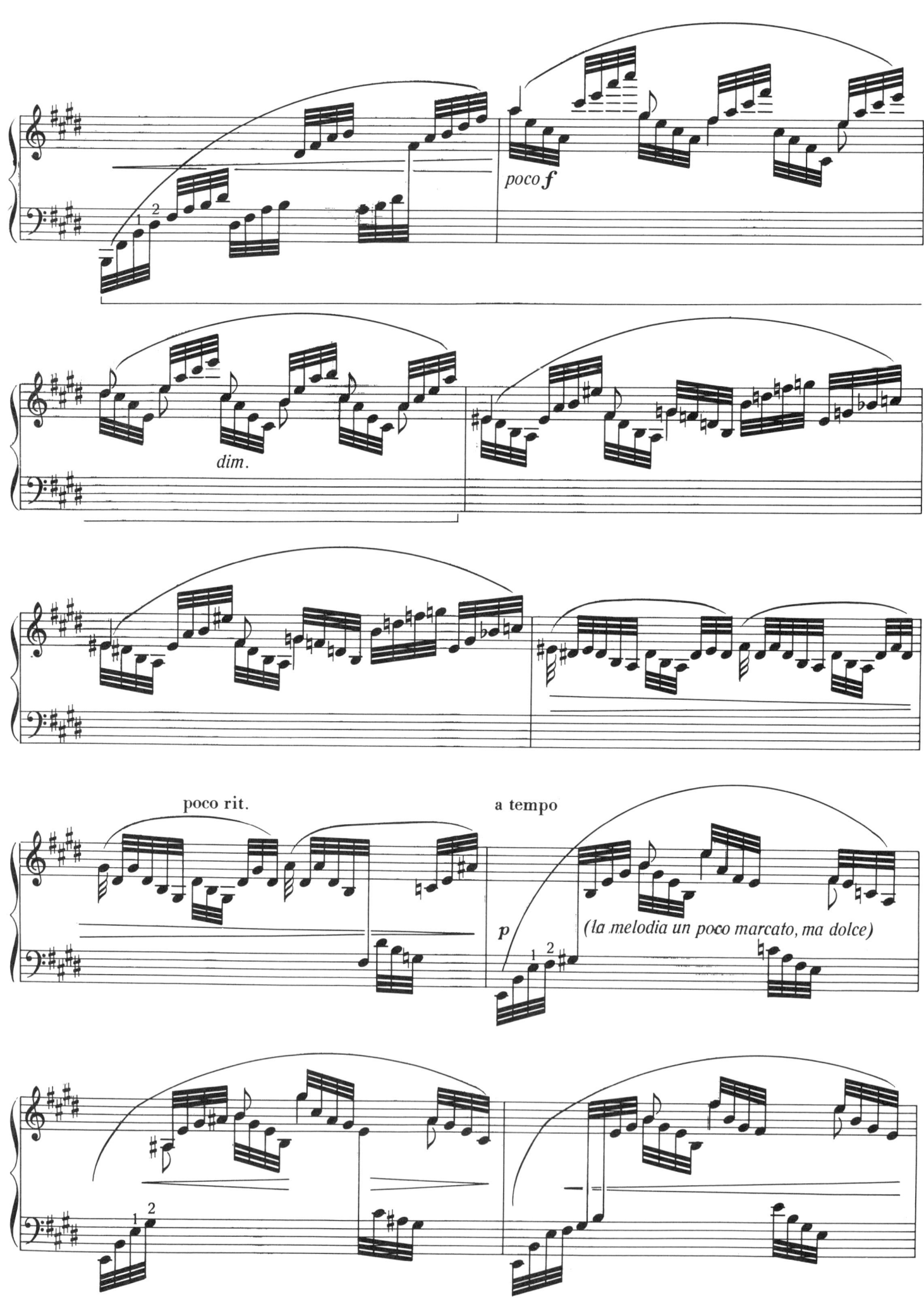

194 *Six Etudes* (Op. 28)

Six Etudes (Op. 28)

Six Etudes (Op. 28)

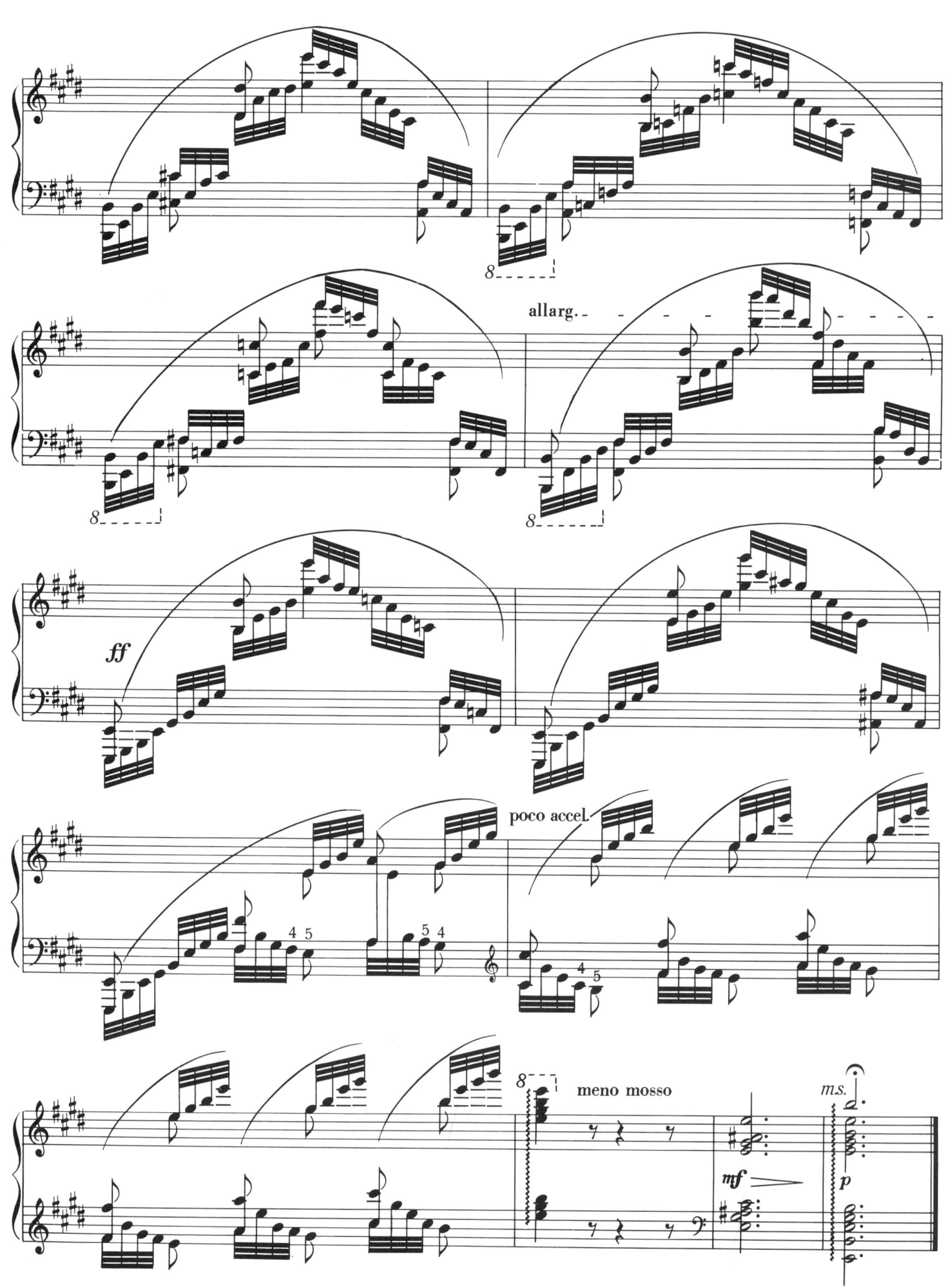

Six Etudes (Op. 28)

Capriccio in F Minor
Etude, Op. 28, No. 6 (1916)

Six Etudes (Op. 28)

Six Etudes (Op. 28)

204 *Six Etudes* (Op. 28)

Six Etudes (Op. 28)

206 *Six Etudes* (Op. 28)

Six Etudes (Op. 28)

Variationen
über ein ungarisches Volkslied
Variations on a Hungarian folk song
Op. 29 (1917)

Var. II

Variations (Op. 29) 211

212 Variations (Op. 29)

Variations (Op. 29)

Variations (Op. 29)

Var. VI

Variations (Op. 29)

Variations (Op. 29)

Variations (Op. 29)

Variations (Op. 29)

Variations (Op. 29)

Pastorale

"Mennyből az angyal"

Pastorale on the Hungarian Christmas song
"The angel is from heaven"

(1920)

Pastorale

224 Pastorale

Pastorale

226 Pastorale

Pastorale

Pastorale

230 *Pastorale*

Pastorale